Winning Resources and Support

OU Business School

Book 5
Managing Resources Effectively

Prepared for the Course Team by Jill Mordaunt, Terry O'Sullivan and Rob Paton

COURSE TEAM

Dr Terry O'Sullivan, *Course Chair*

Barry Jones, *Course Manager*

Sue Treacy, *Course Team Assistant*

Sam Cooper, *OU Business School Regional Coordinator*

Joan Hunt, *OU Business School Regional Manager*

Amanda Shepard, *Institute of Fundraising*

Production Team

Simon Ashby, *Editor*

Paul Beeby, *Media Project Manager*

Martin Brazier, *Graphic Designer*

Holly Clements, *Picture research and Rights clearance*

Roy Lawrence, *Graphic Artist*

David Richings, *Materials procurement*

Critical Readers

Sam Cooper, *Programme Coordinator*

Gail Devlin-Jones, *Eranda Foundation*

Chris Durkin, *University of Northampton*

Acknowledgements

We are grateful to the Institute of Fundraising for its assistance in the development of this course. The course team would like to acknowledge the contribution of the following authors whose work, ideas and creativity in previous courses have helped shape the thinking behind B625 Winning Resources and Support:

Julian Batsleer

Chris Cornforth

Jane Isaacs

Sarabajaya Kumar

Jill Mordaunt

Rob Paton

Alan Thomas

Sue Ward

The Open University
Walton Hall, Milton Keynes
MK7 6AA

First published 2007.

Edited and designed by The Open University.

Typeset in India by Alden Prepress Services, Chennai.

Printed and bound in the United Kingdom by Thanet Press Limited, Margate, Kent.

978 0 7492 2399 1

1.1

CONTENTS

INTRODUCTION TO BOOK 5

No matter how good and exciting your ideas about how to raise money or other kinds of support, these may all come to nothing if you do not manage the process efficiently and effectively. Although we have emphasised the importance of managing fundraising throughout this course, this book in particular focuses on some of the *management* techniques you may wish to use to ensure that your organisation gets the best out of its resources. The key resources that you have to manage are information, people, and finance, and the first three sessions deal with these aspects of management. The final aspect of management discussed is evaluation. Book 5 has four main aims:

- to provide frameworks for managing
- to examine the skills involved in managing people in a fundraising context
- to outline the key elements of budgeting and costing, and ways of assessing financial performance
- to outline the role of evaluation in fundraising.

Session 1 looks at the principles and issues surrounding information management and considers how to make the most effective use of this resource, with a particular focus on environmental scanning, information flow and the use of computerised databases and mailing lists.

Session 2 looks at some of the general management concepts that apply in fundraising: particularly the factors that may motivate and demotivate paid staff and volunteers, how groups and teams work, and some of the problems that may arise in groups that can make them difficult to manage.

Session 3 takes you through the basics of costing for budgets and cash management and explores the issues involved in allocating overheads. It then goes on to examine ways of evaluating financial performance.

Session 4 takes up the topic of evaluation, covering a number of measures which can be used to learn from and improve fundraising activities.

Session 1

Managing Information

CONTENTS

1 MANAGING INFORMATION

1.1 INTRODUCTION

Information management is all about acquiring and storing information so that you and others in your organisation can recall, search and sort it in a variety of ways that will assist in different aspects of winning resources and support. Information is one of an organisation's most important resources. It plays a crucial role in fundraising – particularly in developing relationships with donors, supporters and other organisations.

Much of our discussion in this session will assume the use of computer-based information systems. However, our main concern will be with the general principles, possibilities and issues that surround information.

Aims and learning outcomes

This session has the following aims:

- to alert you to the importance of information management
- to illuminate the main issues associated with gathering, storing, accessing and using a range of information for different purposes
- to consider in what ways an organisation might develop and manage its information systems.

After completing this session you will be able to:

- explain the importance of information gathering and management in winning resources
- carry out simple environmental scanning
- describe some of the main issues involved in gathering, storing and accessing information for different purposes
- outline in general terms how an organisation uses, or could use, databases in the effective management of its information
- discuss what constitutes good quality information and what challenges an organisation faces in this respect
- identify and build on your own experience and competence in information management.

ACTIVITY 1.1

Which of the following do you do systematically, and which could you do better? Write brief notes indicating which are relevant for you personally, and whether you are content with how you do things at the moment.

Storing business cards:

_____

_____

_____

Filing correspondence:

_____

_____

_____

Circulating newsletters and conference or workshop information:

_____

_____

_____

Sharing information on an intranet:

_____

_____

_____

Scanning and storing publications (whether in print, broadcast or web-based):

_____

_____

_____

Storing lists of participants from conferences or events you attend or organise:

_____

_____

_____

Using an email program to manage information on contacts, and to store and retrieve important correspondence:

_____

_____

_____

Storing notes of meetings and conversations in a personal organiser, diary or notebook:

_____

_____

_____

Recalling names and faces:

_____

_____

_____

Keeping computerised lists and databases:

_____

_____

_____

These are just some of the ways that information (some of it important, some of it less so) comes into your working life. Some of the items may not be particularly problematic for you, or your role. Others, such as managing contact information using an email program, can lead to significant savings in time and effort with a little more technical knowledge and application. The point about information management is that such savings of time and effort will have an effect not just on your own efficiency, but on the quality and clarity of the information you can pass on to colleagues and others outside the organisation involved in your information flows.

1.2 DATA AND INFORMATION

Market researchers often talk about 'raw' data, meaning the unprocessed sets of numbers or words which they collect in the course of survey research. The image is a useful one when we make the distinction between data and information. Just as the raw ingredients of a meal need to be cooked and combined before they can be made edible, so the raw materials of data (the disconnected numbers, words and signs that surround us in any organisation) need to be analysed and interpreted before they can become useful information. Information is data that has been transformed in a way which allows it to communicate knowledge or meaning to its receiver. To put it another way, information is data which has been made useful.

Of course, because interpretation is involved, misunderstandings can occur. In the same way that effective communication relies on sharing a common language with whomever you are trying to communicate, so the effective sharing of information requires you to consider your audience. It may be that what is clearly information to you (because you are familiar with its context and meaning) is still only data to a recipient. A good example of this is the way in which numbers can be presented to a board of trustees. You as a fundraiser might be perfectly comfortable with a computer printout showing numbers which you can combine by eye if necessary, and which are identified by abbreviated labels. Your trustees, on the other hand, might only understand this information if it is aggregated properly, tabulated clearly (perhaps with year-on-year comparisons and percentages to show trends) and labelled in an explicitly meaningful way.

Much of the information you provide as a fundraiser will be in the service of a case for support. Sometimes the way in which you provide such information will be out of your direct control – such as on a grant application form, where the grant-giving body has structured the questions and layout in order to facilitate comparisons with other applicants. You may consider that this limits your freedom to present information in the most relevant or eloquent way. However, it also creates the opportunity for you to learn and use information conventions used by grant-givers (and thus write more effective applications). When you can exercise more control over the way in which you present information (for example, when making a presentation to a group) remember that both rational and emotional appeals count. Statistics which are memorable and dramatic will make your case more meaningful – another example of the power of turning data into information. Considering the needs of your audience prevents overloading them with information, just as thinking about who needs to know what, and why, can reduce overload inside your organisation.

Information can help you make better decisions, but cannot make decisions for you. This is a good maxim to bear in mind when thinking about managing information. For example, decisions about which fundraising techniques to use will be more likely to lead to success if you know how cost-effective such techniques have proven in the past. At the same time, you need to make a judgement as to how likely such success is to repeat itself, in what may be changed circumstances. Furthermore, management decisions are taken within a limited timeframe. The amount of information you can incorporate in any decision is almost always going to be less than you would ideally like. Again, this means that an element of judgement is inevitable. It also means that the quality of your information needs to be as high as possible.

1.2.1 Information flow

Thinking about the way in which it flows into, around and out of an organisation is a good first step in any attempt to manage information more effectively. Even though fundraisers and campaigners often appear to be working in isolation from colleagues who are providing the services which the organisation offers, there is a sense in which every member of an organisation is part of an interlinked flow of information – some of it coming from outside, some of it originating internally and some of it passing back out again.

For example, fundraisers exchange information with donors and supporters outside the organisation. The fundraisers offer information about the good cause and opportunities to help in order to mobilise supporters and motivate donors or funders. In return they receive information about what techniques work in particular contexts, what kind of activities inspire and sustain their supporter base, and details of the policies leading to support from institutions such as businesses or government agencies.

With certain exceptions, the information flowing out of the organisation from the fundraisers will not have originated with them as individuals. They will have received it in the form of needs, priorities and agreed targets communicated from senior management. They will, however, have selected from it and shaped it to what they perceive will meet the needs of local fundraising groups or contacts in local authorities or other grant-making bodies. Similarly, the information from supporters will flow back into the organisation through the fundraising function – either as formal results, expressed in numbers, or as softer, but no less important, information about what excites donors and what may be turning them off. Again, this will not travel through the fundraising department unmediated. Selectivity, different interpretations, forgetting, delays and embellishment are all inevitable in human systems of communication. This will always remain a challenge in information management – but being conscious of it should help us ask the right questions in thinking about getting information to flow through our organisations in the most effective way.

Consider the many different groups who require information from a fundraiser. Clearly, information flows are not just one-way, but for the purposes of developing your competency in information management we will concentrate to begin with, on the responsibility you have to provide information to others. See Figure 1.1.

The figure shows various groups whose needs that affect information management. Of course there are times when you need to supply information on a one-off basis (for example, to a journalist with a question about a particular event or issue), but the main focus of information management is the regular information that helps people inside and outside an organisation to carry out their responsibilities, and to maintain more effective links between the organisation and its stakeholders (Hibberd and Evatt, 2004).

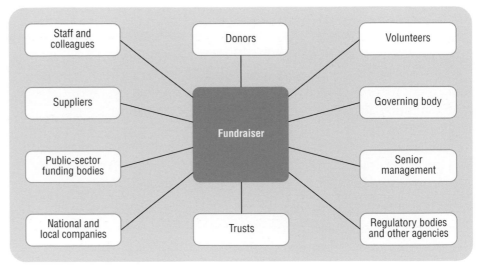

Figure 1.1 Different groups whose information needs a fundraiser may have to consider

---

ACTIVITY 1.2

Draw a version of Figure 1.1 that is adapted to your own situation. Indicate on the arrows leading to each group or individual the main types of information they require from you.

There may be marked similarities between these groups and their needs, but the important thing to take from this exercise is an awareness of which stakeholders need what information to enhance the effectiveness of your links.

Choices about what information an organisation needs to communicate, and how it communicates it, depend not only on the needs of stakeholders, such as the ones you have been exploring in Activity 1.2, but also on a number of factors related to the organisation itself. These include:

- *the management style* (especially how open and consultative the organisational culture is)
- the *urgency* with which the information needs to be communicated
- the *complexity* of the information
- the *sensitivity* of the information (i.e. the impact that losses or inaccuracies in the information would have on the organisation's operations) and the range of people to whom it is relevant
- the *need to keep a record* of the communication
- whether the organisation is *geographically concentrated* or spread out across a number of locations (if spread out more effort and thought may be needed to keep colleagues informed)
- the communications *options available* (which might include memos, noticeboards, team meetings, one-to-one meetings, telephone and email).

There are also intriguing political undertones in much information sharing. If 'knowledge itself is power' (as the seventeenth-century English essayist Francis Bacon wrote) you might well expect it to be jealously guarded. Secrecy and information hoarding is often a sign that an individual, or an organisation, is under threat. But when the control of information becomes dominated by internal politics rather than the needs of service-users (or, in the context of fundraising, the needs of supporters and donors) the result is a steep decline in organisational effectiveness. Properly considered approaches to managing the flow of information to and from the fundraising function should help counteract this problem, but – particularly in organisations which are working under pressure with stretched resources – it is an issue which needs to be kept under constant review.

1.2.2 Environmental Scanning

One of the biggest problems with information is that there is so much of it. Information of all kinds, some of it valuable, some of it entirely irrelevant, surrounds us on all sides in the external environment. But scanning the environment for what may be useful indicators of the changing threats and opportunities that face a fundraising organisation remains more of an art than a science. There are no simple formulas for how it should be done. Therefore, the intention of this section is to help you increase your awareness of how you undertake environmental scanning at present, so that you are in a better position to reflect on and improve your own practice of information gathering.

One of the difficulties of environmental scanning is that relevant information may be gleaned from so many different sources: newspapers, the internet, television, radio, professional journals, research reports, conferences and events, personal contacts and so on. This means that environmental scanning is not something that you can sit down and do once every month; it is a matter of constantly keeping an eye open for information that might be relevant. Activity 1.3 should help you think about how you go about environmental scanning.

It is often difficult to judge how useful a particular source of information is going to be. Since there are numerous sources of information, anyone involved in environmental scanning is faced with a dilemma. If your efforts are focused too narrowly you may miss vital information. However, to spread your focus too widely may require too much time and energy, or mean that you become swamped with information and unable to see the wood for the trees.

ACTIVITY 1.3

List under the following headings the various sources of information that you have used over the last year to keep in touch with developments that might affect the work of your group or organisation. Then indicate how often you use the source, the types of information sought and how useful the information has been in influencing the strategy or plans of your group or organisation. The first row has been filled in as an example.

Information source	Frequency	Information sought	Usefulness
Professional publications			
Funding for Change	*Scan every four months when published*	*Changes of priorities or personnel which might indicate new fundraising opportunities.*	*Occasional useful information.*
Searching the Internet			
Newspapers			
Conferences, workshops and other events			
Television and radio			
Personal contacts and networks			
Other			

It is surprising how much useful information can be picked up by what seem to be chance or accidental discoveries. This involves never quite leaving the job – being alert to the possibilities of information that you glean at a party or in a chance conversation.

Another problem facing anyone trying to make sense of their environment is that the information they receive may be ambiguous. Information may conflict, be uncertain or inaccurate; you only have to look at areas such as economic forecasting to know how often predictions turn out to be wrong. Working out strategy often involves making decisions based on information that is confusing and uncertain.

In addition it is important to remember that perception is not a passive process. We actively seek out and interpret information; and what we see is influenced by our existing values and beliefs. As a result we are all, to some extent, blinkered in our attempts to make sense of the world. In particular we often find it easier to 'not see' or ignore information that challenges cherished views. The danger of course is that we may miss, ignore or misinterpret vital information. An ability to keep an open mind and to question beliefs and assumptions is important to the success of environmental scanning and for planning strategy.

Environmental scanning can provide you with advance warning about what are likely to be the important factors affecting your organisation. Such understanding begins with spotting patterns in events and, in particular, identifying new patterns as things change. It is an area where you will need to use your own judgement and draw on your past experience.

1.2.3 What makes for good quality information?

But what criteria can we apply to evaluating information from environmental scanning or any other source (especially in view of our efforts to review and improve the information we provide to others)?

In some people's minds there is a prejudice against certain types of information as being 'soft' rather than 'hard'. Hard information is objective and is usually expressed in numbers. It has scientific authority (and can be very useful in making cases). It includes results, statistics, process specifications, numerical trends and so on. It is often overemphasised in such things as government targets as it is easily quantified. Soft information is qualitative – it includes estimates, feelings, opinions and judgements. The key question is not whether information is hard or soft, but how good its quality is. We propose quality criteria for information of any kind. Having listed them here, we will discuss them with reference to their implications for winning resources. Good quality information should be:

1 relevant

2 clear

3 sufficiently accurate

4 complete

5 trustworthy

6 concise

7 timely

8 communicated to the right person

9 communicated via the right channel

10 cost-effective.

Relevance

Irrelevant information is the visible symptom of information overload. It needs deleting, binning or preventative measures if it is not to clog up your in-tray (or in-box) and perhaps obscure what is actually relevant to your job. Sometimes you will have to waste precious time working your way through information to extract the occasional relevant nugget – for example, when doing environmental scanning. Information and communication technology can give you some control over receiving and passing on information in a way which highlights relevance. Email lists, for example, often allow you to specify which particular topics you are interested in, and you can target information as you pass it on by using a number of selective distribution lists to limit the circulation of some documents while making others available universally. Or you can ensure that information is available on demand by storing computer files in a central storage area and allowing colleagues to access them as and when required.

Clarity

This is particularly important in the context of winning resources and support. If your message to potential sources of support is not understood it will not be effective – and the same is true of any internal message aimed at gaining cooperation.

Data can often be transformed into information by being presented clearly. Consider the following presentation of a basic statistic, for example. In 2004/5 the total amount donated to charity by individual givers in the UK was £8.2 billion. This is an impressive number but not much use on its own. A clearer, and more vivid, way of expressing the same statistic is that the average monthly contribution per adult member of the UK population is £14.17, but that only 57% of the population participate in giving in any four week period (NCVO/CAF, 2006). This puts rather a different spin on the data – emphasising the need (and potential) to widen the circle of donors.

Accuracy and precision

The costs of generating and obtaining information are generally in proportion to its accuracy. For example, you might be able to find out a lot about attitudes to affinity cards among people who resemble your supporters from published information. Finding out what your supporters themselves think about affinity cards would involve the expensive step of conducting primary research. This would certainly give you more accurate information, but would the extra expense be worth it? You might be able to improve decisions about launching such a card just as effectively by using the more approximate information gathered from secondary sources (i.e. existing information). There will, of course, be many instances when a higher level of accuracy is essential – but it is worth bearing in mind that delaying a decision in anticipation of further and better information may mean that the opportunity to which it relates passes.

Precision refers to the amount of detail included in the information. In budgeting, for example, it may be that at a strategic planning level figures can be rounded to the nearest 1,000 currency units; whereas in operational planning the level of detail needs to be down to 100s or even 10s. As with accuracy, the more precise the information, the greater the cost of providing it.

Completeness

Perhaps sufficiency or adequacy would be a better term here, because there is no such thing as complete information. What you need to receive, or to make available to others, is enough information to make a decision or carry out a task. For example, if you are briefing a designer with a view to preparing some promotional material, the more information you can provide (details about the target audience, the good cause, the event, suggested images, even a mocked-up rough) the more confident the designer will be in producing something which you will be able to approve.

Trustworthiness

The reliability of your information depends to some extent on how critical you are of its source. The internet, for example, is a marvellous source of information about all sorts of issues which affect winning resources and support, but websites need to be treated with caution. In other forms of publishing, such as books, newspapers, magazines and broadcasting, there are levels of editorial control through which the material must be filtered before making it into the public domain. This acts as a form of quality control. No such filters exist on the internet so it is important to evaluate the source of the information. You might, for example, be researching a presentation on an issue of concern to your organisation. Websites from government departments, companies and pressure groups may all have useful information to contribute – but each will be promoting its own agenda so the information provided will be partial (both in the sense of being committed to a particular position and in the sense of being incomplete).

Useful principles here are to choose sources which have proved reliable in the past, and to check your findings from one source against accounts of the same phenomenon from others so that you get a balanced view. It is also worth indicating, in information you pass on, what level of confidence you have in it. Marketing research agencies do this as a matter of course with their findings using statistical procedures. Less scientifically, but still very usefully, terms like 'best case' or 'worst case' can help users interpret the reliability of a particular forecast.

Conciseness

Time and attention span dictate that the more concise the information you receive and produce the more likely it is to be used productively. This explains the popularity of the report format for documents that disseminate information within organisations. Brevity is one of the advantages of this way of writing which can be extended to emails and memos. Keeping communications as short as possible has the further advantage of concentrating the writer's mind on the important points, thus prioritising key information.

A practical way of avoiding excessive regular information from silting up internal systems is to use the principle of 'exception reporting'. This is based on the idea that 'no news is good news' – in other words a report is only supplied if something is wrong and needs attention. This can dramatically reduce the amount of information which managers need to deal with, but it also places considerable responsibility on people throughout the organisation to recognise and articulate problems in time for something to be done about them.

Timeliness

Decisions take place in a limited timeframe. If the purpose of information is to improve decision making it needs to be available in time to be acted on. Relating this to the model of the control loop, or the version of it we call the fundraising cycle, information for monitoring the performance of planned activity on a regular basis needs to be available in step with meetings where such performance is monitored. This may seem glaringly obvious but, rather like cash flow, the actual times at which information flows come on-stream are sometimes overlooked. Being realistic in advance about how much information, and of what kind, to use for monitoring and evaluation can help you to anticipate and avoid this problem. Timeliness in provision of information to external contacts can include keeping them informed of new initiatives or policies from an early stage of development. Many voluntary organisations and charities have an open, consultative culture where a wide range of internal and external stakeholders help shape such developments through their ideas and advice.

Communication to the right person

Familiarity with roles and authority within the organisation is essential if you are to maximise the effectiveness of the information you pass on. A fundraiser or campaigner needs to be a visible presence in an organisation so that people at all levels can pass information on to you. This is particularly true if your role encompasses responsibility for media relations. Becoming a familiar face around the organisation may give you access to information on which to base attractive press stories which would remain undiscovered were you to spend all day in your own office.

Communication via the right channel

How you communicate information is another key quality issue. Considering the preferences and needs of your recipient is as important here as in any other form of communication. External audiences such as donors and supporters are likely to connect more directly with non-technical information expressed in lay terms. Internal colleagues, for the most part, will have a greater capacity to understand more complex and specialised information. Finally, for all the sophistication of modern office technology, word of mouth is still one of the most important channels available for communicating information. It is particularly good for reaching senior managers who, according to a classic piece of management research, spend most of their time talking and listening to people (Mintzberg, 1973).

Cost-effectiveness

The effort of gathering, interpreting, storing and disseminating information costs a great deal in terms of time and organisational resources. Information only repays this effort by improving the quality of decisions. The value that it adds – for example, enabling you to target donors effectively – needs to outweigh its costs. Sometimes these costs are easily identifiable, as for example the expense of installing and maintaining a sophisticated database. Sometimes they are more difficult to pin down, but no less real for that.

A useful idea here is that of 'opportunity cost'. The time and resources spent gathering, processing and transferring information cannot be applied to other urgent priorities. A strategic approach to deciding what information you and your colleagues really need should take this into account. Does your department or organisation produce information which nobody ever uses? It would not be unique if it did – but the effort spent producing it would be better applied elsewhere.

ACTIVITY 1.4

Think of a regular item of information that a fundraiser might provide to an internal stakeholder such as a manager or colleague, or to a key external stakeholder group such as donors. Or, if you prefer, think of a source of information that you use regularly (such as a particular website, or a trade publication). Using the following form, rate it against each of the information quality criteria on a scale of 1 to 5, where 5 ➡

indicates excellent performance against the criterion and 1 indicates poor performance against the criterion. In the third column list changes that could improve the quality of the information as appropriate.

Information quality criterion	Rating (1–5)	Possible changes
Relevance		
Clarity		
Accuracy and precision		
Completeness		
Trustworthiness		
Conciseness		
Timeliness		
Communication to the right person		
Communication via the right channel		
Cost-effectiveness		

You may be surprised at the results of your reflections. It could be useful to ask a colleague to make a similar assessment of the same piece of information.

1.2.4 Information ownership

Information, as we have seen, is a valuable resource in the right hands. Its loss or inaccuracy can have a negative impact on the operations of the organisation (the quality of 'sensitivity' mentioned earlier). It follows that information needs to be properly maintained and managed like any valuable asset – in the sense of being regularly updated and protected.

Protection involves making information safe against accidental loss (or even sabotage). Backing-up valuable information is a relatively straightforward procedure when using computer storage. For paper-based files it means secure storage and archiving. Important tasks like these need to be built into a routine where they happen as a matter of course.

Protection also means keeping information confidential. Any attempt to manage information needs to consider carefully who ought to have access to what. While avoiding unnecessary restrictions, it makes sense to limit the availability of information to those who need to know it. The inappropriate disclosure of information has an adverse effect on the organisation's operations (for example, leaking news about a new initiative will lead to its planned media launch losing impact). More importantly there are legal implications to the collection, storage and processing of personal data such as the names, addresses and details on a donor database. Individuals still own the information you have on them, and, under the provisions of data protection legislation in many countries, they can demand to see it.

UK data protection legislation provides that personal data kept by organisations should be adequate, relevant, accurate and not excessive, and that it should not be kept for longer than is necessary. Any organisation involved in data processing has to notify the relevant government authority (the Information Commissioner in the UK) and specify what kind of data is involved and for what purposes (http://www.ico.gov.uk). Similar principles apply in many other countries.

A data controller for each organisation has to be named. This individual has final responsibility for the collation, security, accuracy and use of information. This need not be someone in the fundraising function itself, but it clearly needs to be someone with whom fundraisers are in close contact.

Concerns over data protection have arisen because of the power of information and communication technology to collect, combine and manipulate information in ways which are potentially invasive of individual privacy. Used responsibly, such technology provides fundraisers with tools to build close relationships with a potentially enormous body of donors and supporters. It is to this that we now turn in the next section.

1.3 DATABASES AND DONORS

Databases lie at the heart of many aspects of fundraising: from your network of contacts and supporters, to detailed analyses of market research preferences that might indicate whether someone is likely to donate to your cause, or lists of addresses of particular types of organisations and groups. Some organisations exist merely to collect and sell this kind of information. This section examines, in as non-technical a way as possible, some of the ways in which databases may be used to support your work.

1.3.1 Computers and donor/supporter development

At its simplest, a database is just a list of consistently structured records. The address section at the back of a diary is a good example. Each record is in a standard format and allows information to be stored and retrieved easily. The fact that the entries in the address section are in alphabetical order helps you to locate the person you are looking for, and the fact that each contains a space for a telephone number, email and postal address means that you are confident of finding what you need.

Computers take this simple idea of a list several steps forward. Instead of having to store the information in alphabetical order of surname it can be located against a number of criteria which the user can set. Instead of spaces on a paper page to record things like telephone numbers the computerised database has fields in each record which together can store huge amounts of data. Not only first names or phone numbers, but details of transactions, records of contact, demographic details – the list is almost infinitely extendable. Essential fields for fundraising databases concern the *frequency*, *recency* and *value* of donations. Anything else that indicates the level of commitment (such as attending a meeting or serving on a committee) and the particular interests of your supporters – especially the comments they make – will also be important.

The computer's ability to cross reference, sort, compare and combine information on the basis of these fields is what makes the database such a powerful tool. It effectively transforms it from a database into an 'information base' – a system for tracking and enhancing relationships with donors.

Because they handle large numbers of records quickly, computer-based information systems allow you to do things that would otherwise be impossible or impractical. But the things they do with the records they hold are basically simple and familiar – they search, they select, they sort, they count and they compare. Of course, they can only do all these in relation to the information that they hold. So, for example, if the records do not include information on when a person last made a donation (or, to be more technical about it, if this was not one of the *fields* specified when the system was being set up) then there is no way the computer can recognise lapsed donors. With that crucial proviso, the computer's ability to sift and sort means that you can do the following things with a list of supporters' records:

- *Segmentation* – You can divide the list into different categories of supporter and target your appeals to them accordingly.

- *Monitoring and analysis* – You can see how different types of supporter responded to an appeal or, by comparing responses over time, you can spot trends that might otherwise go unnoticed. For example, a falling response rate to your appeals and a slowly dwindling band of supporters might be masked by the fact that those who remained were being more generous.

- *Testing and research* – You can try out different ideas for an appeal to see which works best. A so-called 'split run' test involves sending two different mailings to matched samples drawn from your list. Then you can use the more successful version for the main mailing to everyone else.

The computer is thus a powerful tool for donor development – understanding your supporters better, responding to them appropriately and drawing them on to higher levels of commitment. It can also provide a series of financial and management reports based on response rates. More recent database applications can integrate fundraising activity with other aspects of an organisation's operation, to form a tapestry of information that has the potential to help the organisation improve service delivery, learn more powerfully from its experience and communicate more accurately to funders, boards and the people they serve.

It is tempting when thinking about databases to focus on the technology rather than the way in which it is used. After all, computers can do remarkable things. However, the human factor is what counts. No matter how sophisticated your technology, the culture and effectiveness of your organisation will dictate how well the resulting information is used. The example in Box 1.1 illustrates these issues.

BOX 1.1

GALA PERFORMANCE

The Gay and Lesbian Choruses (GALA Choruses) is an organisation providing professional development for artists and managers, capacity-building services, events, conferences and networking. The organisation originally operated from an office in Washington DC staffed by three paid workers, but it now combines that base with a more geographically dispersed network of three further staff working from home offices based in Florida. A grant from the DC Commission on Arts and Humanities has helped develop technology in support of its work.

Discussions with a consultant led to the conclusion that the main priority for development was GALA's five-year-old members' database. This had served the organisation well when first installed on a single site, but it was causing problems now that its activities had spread. Remote workers were unable to access the database yet needed the information. The operations director in Washington was having to generate reports from the system and then fax them through to colleagues in Florida. The inefficiencies this created were considerable, and the team started to consider the available options. These included investing in a new system, or choosing an Application Service Provider (ASP) solution which would effectively put their database on the internet where it could be accessed from any location they chose.

Instead of jumping to any conclusions, however, the team decided to map the information flows to and from the members' database and between the DC and Florida offices. They thought hard about the kinds of reports they would need from the membership database to make effective and timely decisions. They also worked through the questions of who should have access to which parts of the information, given its confidentiality, and who should be able to edit and add to the database.

The somewhat surprising conclusion they reached was that, far from needing a new database system, what they really needed was proper training throughout the organisation on what they had already. With a few upgrades here and there the current system did actually serve their needs. The information-flow mapping process led to a peer-training strategy whereby the operations manager shared expertise with other members of the organisation and developed training materials and a manual for permanent reference. By focusing their thinking on their data needs, rather than the data tools available, GALA Choruses staff were able to make strategic decisions which increased staff buy-in to their information management and developed organisational learning.

(Source: adapted from Kanter, 2002)

Most organisations will already have some kind of fundraising database like this. However, organisations and their needs develop. So does what is available. The computer industry itself moves very quickly. Hardware and software date rapidly. This means that, even though in the voluntary sector expense is always going to be an issue, spending on new and improved database systems (for the increased efficiency and effectiveness they bring) is likely to be a high priority. It might be that you have outgrown your present system or are frustrated by the poor support the supplier can offer. While it is beyond the scope of this book to cover the details of specifying or commissioning database systems, the following general principles (Flory, 2001) apply not only to developing your resources in hardware and software, but also to the wider issues of information management in general:

- define, agree and record your objectives
- define your requirements and allocate priorities

- define your criteria accordingly, and try before you buy
- check suppliers carefully, take up references and see the systems in action
- plan, budget and monitor – look three years ahead
- ensure system continuity and retain knowledge – document your procedures carefully so that staff changes or illness do not imperil your information management
- make sure you have someone who understands databases in the organisation, or use a consultant.

Flory also points out that it is important not only to invest in the hardware and software itself but to make adequate provision for training, system implementation, the cost of converting any data across from existing systems and project management:

> A good rule of thumb is to double the initial licence cost in order to arrive at a total first year cost. From year two onwards there will be a maintenance cost that ranges from 12 to 20 per cent of the initial licence cost (assuming you don't have any on-going training!).

> (Flory, 2001)

So, information management is a major area of investment in winning resources and support. The costs involved should provide an incentive for organisations to think carefully about exactly what they need, as well as encouraging them to protect and maintain the costly results.

1.3.2 The information industry

The widespread adoption of database technology has driven rapid expansion in the use of 'database marketing' by all sorts of organisations to develop relationships with customers based on developing knowledge of them. Direct mail is one of its most visible manifestations, whereby individuals are sent information and offers by a wide range of organisations. In the UK charities are second only to financial services in the amount of direct mail items they send each year. The industry that produces and handles these mailings is made up of several different sorts of specialist agency. These include marketing agencies that develop the ideas; designers, copywriters and printers that produce the materials; mailing houses that actually pack and dispatch the envelopes; and agencies that process the replies. But for present purposes, the most important are the *list brokers* – who buy, sell and rent lists of names – and the *computer bureaux* with massive database systems offering a range of information services including *suppression*, *profiling* and *data enhancement*. Happily, the mystery lies mainly in the jargon; the ideas themselves are simple.

If you want to sell, raise money or campaign through the post, one of the first things you need is a list of names. These lists are created in many different ways: from publicly available information (e.g. the electoral roll), from responses to campaigns or offers (including membership drives), and from market research.

The creators of such lists in the UK must register under the Data Protection Act and collect data fairly. For example, people on lists must have been offered an opt-out if they would prefer not to be contacted.

The list industry comprises a number of different types of company. *List owners* are generators of mailing lists, either specifically for rental or to support their own businesses (such as publishing, selling through the mail, or having a membership). This means that practically every voluntary organisation or charity is itself a list owner with the potential to make an income from this asset alone. *List managers* take on the job of selling mailing lists on behalf of a list owner. They act simply like a hired-in sales and marketing department and are paid a management fee by the list owner. *List brokers* are the people you are likely to deal with in your search for suitable new prospects to mail. They buy lists on behalf of clients just as an advertising agency buys space in a newspaper. And, like an advertising agency, they offer impartial advice, research, recommendation of options and evaluation of results. The final similarity to an advertising agency is that list brokers are paid by commission based on the price you pay to rent the list owner's list.

One of the most important things the list broker can advise on is the *profile* (that is to say, the broad characteristics) of the people on the list – in terms of their socio-economic group, age or interests – so you can select the lists that are most likely to contain a high proportion of people interested in the material you will send them. And if you are not sure, you can test a sample of the list to see what the response is like.

A list acquired in this way is known as a *cold* list, in contrast to the *warm* list of existing supporters which most organisations will already possess. Responses to a cold list will be far lower – around one per cent is common – but since the aim is to acquire new supporters who will continue to support your cause over a number of years, you may be prepared to invest money in order to build up your list.

Building up your own list on your own database is, of course, the best policy in the long term. Most external lists are available for a one-time mailing use only. Additional uses, such as following up by telephone, have to be agreed in advance. In all cases the list owner (from whom the broker sources the list) retains the copyright of the list. All commercially available lists contain 'seed names' which are actually the addresses of the owner or the owner's agents which means that they automatically know when their list has been used and by whom.

No list is 100 per cent accurate because of the speed with which name and address information goes out of date. Furthermore, combining lists from a number of sources inevitably means that there will be duplication between them, as some of the same names will appear on more than one list. Even within your own list, it is highly possible that duplication will occur (as supporters often forget that they are on lists and ask to be included in mailings). For a potential donor to receive multiple mailings of the same appeal looks very bad for the good cause involved and is, of course, a waste of money and resources. There are also services such as the UK's Mailing Preference Service (MPS) whereby individuals can opt out of direct mailings by expressing their preference not to receive any.

This means that before undertaking a large-scale mailing, using its own list augmented by bought-in lists, an organisation needs to engage the services of a *computer bureau*. Computer bureaux are another important component of the list industry. They provide computer-processing services for third parties, which may include:

- deleting from the new lists all the names that already appear on the existing list (de-duplicating)
- combining the new lists, taking out all the duplication of names in the process (merge/purge processing)
- checking and correcting postcodes and other aspects of the data quality (data enhancement)
- running the new list against the Mailing Preference Service (MPS) list – which allows removal of all the names of those who have registered with the MPS their desire not to receive unsolicited mail
- running the list against a mortality file – which removes the names of recently deceased people – and against a 'gone away' file to cut down on the number of returned items
- by a similar process, removing all the people with bad debts and poor credit references.

This process of removing unwanted names is called *suppression*. It can be extended much further depending on what is known about the sorts of people who are likely to support your cause and the data available. You might, for example, want to delete everyone living in remote rural areas and inner cities; or all men; or everyone under the age of 50; or even all of these categories – if your supporters are primarily older women who live in the suburbs or in towns and villages. Of course, in deleting so many names you are losing some potential supporters, but if it sharply increases your response rate to a cold mailing it will be well worthwhile.

The names and addresses of everyone in the UK – available from the electoral registers – are now held on large commercial databases. Since electoral registers are regularly updated, it is relatively easy to add information on people's length of tenure at their address. To this can be added information from a whole variety of sources about large numbers of people – for example, credit ratings from credit reference bureaux, the information gathered from the guarantee return cards that are provided with a wide range of household goods and, increasingly, the information about preferences and lifestyle that people provide through consumer surveys. All this data can then be further enhanced in a number of ways: geographic information can be added – so that particular postcodes are recorded as being modern and affluent suburban, as older properties or as small towns. Local census data concerning, for example, the age structure of the population in an area can be incorporated. Various sorts of 'probability data' can be added by assuming, for example, that neighbours tend to be alike (so, if you have information about the purchasing patterns or leisure interests of some of the people on a street you can assume that the others will not be so different). Another example is the use of names to help estimate people's age – 'Edith' was common in the UK before the Second World War, 'Jason' is a modern name and so on.

This information is used by the bureau to *profile* your list. Profiles can be based on the *neighbourhood* or *life-stage* (for example, a high concentration of young families with middle incomes); on *lifestyle indicators* such as occupational group, spending patterns and age; or on *interests and attitudes* (technically these are called geo-demographic profiling, sociographic profiling, and psychographic profiling, respectively) or on some combination of these. The result is to give you a greater understanding of the sorts of people who support your cause. The terminology of the industry has now reached everyday language. Do you appeal to the 'yuppie' (young, upwardly-mobile professional) or 'dinky' (double income, no kids yet)? Should you be looking for more 'baby-boomers' (the post-war generation of babies) or concentrating your efforts on 'woopies' (well-off older people)? We might cringe at the stereotypical terminology, but profiling can help our thinking about segmentation at a strategic level.

A bureau may divide the population into as many as 50 different groups. If you then provide a list of your supporters (at least 20,000 names are required for this sort of exercise) the bureau will be able to match your records against those it holds and then describe to you the profiles of your supporters. If your organisation has been doing its job properly it will mainly confirm things you already suspected, but the agency can then also offer you lists of all the other people in the country who have similar profiles – and who are therefore relatively good prospects for cold mailings aimed at building up your list. It has to be said, though, that experts differ over the effectiveness of this approach. Some argue that, in practice, it is no more effective than using a carefully chosen list – but costs much more. For example, if you are searching for people likely to be interested in wildlife conservation charities, then a list of people who subscribed to a newspaper readers' offer for a pair of quality binoculars will probably be as successful as a list created by a sophisticated profiling exercise. The counter-argument is that profiling is a developing art and is becoming ever more refined and discriminating.

The lists held by specialist bureaux and other agencies can also be used to improve or extend the data you already hold – this is known as *data enhancement*. This can be relatively mundane, like correcting errors in postcodes (some are bound to have crept in), or sophisticated, as when potential legacy prospects on your list are identified using geo-demographic or lifestyle data.

ACTIVITY 1.5

The following exercise will help you start thinking in terms of profiles:

Briefly describe the profiles of the three common types of supporter of an organisation of your choice. Use the sorts of characteristics mentioned in the discussion of profiling and any others you consider appropriate.

1 _____

_____

_____

_____

2 _____

_____

_____

_____

3 _____

_____

_____

_____

Now write brief notes on the following questions:

(a) On what information do you base this?

_____

_____

_____

(b) Would other members of the organisation agree?

_____

_____

_____

(c) In terms of profiles, how might the organisation's supporters be changing?

_____

_____

_____

The concept of profiles is important whether or not you are managing a database. It forces us to make explicit our impressions about our supporters. A database allows us to test those impressions and see how well founded they are. In one way or another we need always to check and reconsider such impressions because they can easily become assumptions – and then fixed ideas. Meanwhile, the actual population of your supporters is gradually changing. Exploring the different profiles among your supporters is really a matter of recognising new things that significant numbers of them now have in common.

1.3.3 List maintenance and development

The importance of keeping lists accurate and up to date can hardly be overemphasised. This means recording new information promptly and meticulously, and having the procedures to respond appropriately – thanking a donor, registering a change of address or noting a request not to allow someone's name to be passed on to any other organisation. Carelessness and delays in what is called *data capture* can cause all the familiar failings that give 'junk mail' a bad name. For example, many supporters can be particularly upset if the name of a deceased relative is not removed promptly from a mailing list or if notified changes of address are not activated. Of course, some things always will go wrong – so a procedure for dealing with complaints is essential. For this purpose, the telephone is quick, direct and more personal than a letter.

It costs a lot less to do business with existing customers than with new ones in any market, and fundraising is no exception. Keeping your existing supporters is more important – and cheaper – than recruiting new ones. This is why well-designed *reactivation programmes,* aimed at those whose interest appears to have lapsed, are so important. Nevertheless, most organisations are also interested in recruiting new supporters. Indeed, a powerful economic logic encourages this: once you have invested in the capacity to handle a large number of records, and are printing documents to mail to your supporters, the additional cost of more names on the list is small. The larger the number of active supporters you have, the sooner your investment will be recovered and be generating a surplus.

But how can you acquire more names economically? Buying or renting lists has already been discussed. You should also ensure that you have exploited to the full the information which you already have. Other methods are:

- *'Member get a member' also known as 'friend get a friend'* – This involves asking existing supporters if they can suggest someone else who might be interested in receiving information about your cause and using the contribution multiplier we explained earlier in this course.

- *Newspaper advertisements and 'inserts' in magazines* – These invite a donation and include a reply coupon. Normally advertisements are an expensive way to raise money – but they are still an effective way of acquiring new names. If your cause is in the news, you may be able to raise money as well as acquiring names.

- *Reciprocal mailings* – These involve you swapping your list with that of another organisation whose supporters you believe are likely to be sympathetic to your cause as well. These have proved to be cheap and lucrative for many organisations (providing that the organisations are not in direct competition, and that permission for such use has been given by the data subjects).

- *Collective mailings* – Some organisations sell space in an envelope that they are mailing to particular lists. This means the cost of the mailing is shared and the people on the list receive information from several organisations simultaneously. For example the Royal Society for the Protection of Birds sends a quarterly magazine to its one million members – a potentially useful outlet for other wildlife charities.

- *Involvement in your activities, promotions and events* – These will not just attract your existing supporters: the names on a petition, the names of those who responded to a joint promotion (for example, on a cereal packet) or who put their names on raffle tickets or in an attendance book, may all be useful additions to your prospect list. Of course, any form or coupon used in this way must allow the individual to opt out of any further mailings.

1.4 PROSPECT RESEARCH

Prospect research is about searching for good prospects – in other words, tracking down the right people to ask. These will be people who are likely to agree to help your cause in an important way (with a major donation perhaps, or by chairing a fundraising committee) and who have the concerns, wealth, prestige or social connections to do so. It is also about knowing your prospects, so that you can decide how best to approach them, and knowing what aspects of your work are likely to have a particular appeal for them.

At its most basic, prospect research is a matter of studying relevant information sources such as directories and media reports. But specialist agencies take this much further: they try to identify wealthy people (through records of share ownership for example, or by following the financial press). When they have done so they set about building up a picture of that person's background, business and family connections, and organisational affiliations (clubs, directorships, trusteeships and so on) for among these may be the hook that will allow a particular organisation to land the 'big fish'. If the client organisation comes up with a specification of the sort of person it is looking for, the agencies search their files for prospects. Alternatively, the organisation may bring along the names of those it has identified in its own records as its most generous and committed supporters, to see if the agency can provide further information about them (data enhancement, in effect).

However, it would be misleading to suggest that prospect research is something only specialists do. We can all keep our eyes and ears open, and we can all learn to recognise indications of an opportunity. One of the most fundamental things is simply to inspect your existing list – you may find people with titles, generous supporters with addresses in tax havens like Switzerland or the Channel Islands or the name of someone who might be a celebrity or the spouse of a celebrity. Likewise, you can note potentially relevant information you come across in newspapers or other local information sources. It can be as simple as being aware when you are meeting people and building relationships that they may in future have something to offer your organisation. This means that you should keep a note on your database of the contact details from their business card. Much useful information can also be found quickly using search facilities on the internet by putting your prospect's name into a search engine such as Google.

BOX 1.2

PROMISING PROSPECTS

Originating in the US, the concept of employing a dedicated prospect research professional is still relatively new to UK charities (and an option only available to those of a certain size whose strategy requires it). Universities and a handful of large charities have led the way since the late 1980s; Oxford and Cambridge were early leaders when prospect research operations opened in 1987 and 1989 respectively, soon showing impressive results in terms of the size and frequency of major donations.

The NSPCC (National Society for the Prevention of Cruelty to Children) was a pioneer in the field. To begin with, there was just one researcher, working in the major gifts department. But as the value of research to a number of different fundraising areas began to become obvious, the charity set up an information and research team as a more general resource. The department has now grown to nine people who are closely integrated into the fundraising process. According to Helen Carpenter, business support manager at NSPCC 'NSPCC researchers are recognised as key consultants in the fundraising process, not just information providers.'

(Source: Adapted from Funnell and Darker, 2007, pp. 26–7)

ACTIVITY 1.6

(a) Thinking of your own organisation, or another which you know well, how, specifically, would you describe the sort of prospect(s) you are seeking? The clearer your picture of them, the more likely you are to recognise them.

_____

_____

_____

_____

_____

_____

_____

(b) Write notes on the steps you already take to identify prospects, how they might be improved and the further steps you might take.

_____

_____

_____

_____

_____

_____

_____

_____

_____

The options available to you are likely to be constrained by the available resources – after all, there are only so many reference works or databases to which any organisation can subscribe, in spite of the information explosion which has resulted from the growth of online sources. More important, perhaps, is a consistent orientation to research (whether from formal or informal sources) and an ability to think laterally and creatively about ways of identifying what is relevant.

 1.5 DEVELOPING A MANAGEMENT INFORMATION SYSTEM

We have considered the qualities that information must have in order to be really useful to your organisation in the way it makes decisions, including decisions on how to go about winning resources and support. We have concentrated in particular on the role of computerised databases and how they tie into fundraising techniques, using what you know about your donors and supporters to maximise the benefits of your relationships with them through direct marketing.

These are all aspects of the strategic use of information in an organisation which can be combined to optimise decision making and operations – a management information system, in short. A good definition of a management information system is:

> A system to convert data from internal and external sources into information, and to communicate that information, in an appropriate form, to managers at all levels in all functions to enable them to make timely and effective decisions for planning, directing and controlling the activities for which they are responsible.

(Lucey, 1998, p. 14)

Lucey provides an outline of a management information system (Figure 1.2) which can help us understand information flow for fundraising purposes just as usefully as for any other type of information system in an organisation (such as a payroll system, which not only makes sure that people get paid on time but also provides management with information such as salary costs per department and yearly analyses).

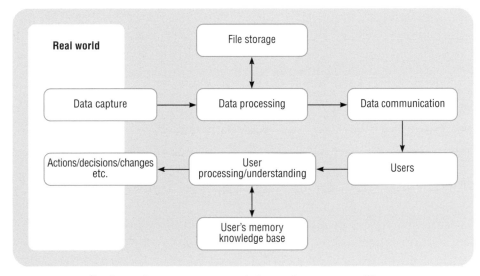

Figure 1.2 Outline of a management information system (Source: Lucey, 1998)

For fundraisers and campaigners data capture can come in many ways – from a form filled out at an event, to a reply from a prospect on a rented list who has received a cold mailing. The data might be in paper form, email or some other electronic format. Making *data capture* a routine part of your system ensures that it can be done reliably and regularly. The next stage – *data processing* – might involve storage for future use or for an active process which, for example, looks to see how many supporters you have in a particular area with a view to forming a group. The results of this database search would be communicated in the form of a report to whoever is responsible for working with groups (*Users* in Figure 1.2). It would need to be communicated using an appropriate form and channel, to enable them to understand it and incorporate it into their learning. It might well be that, with training and sufficiently user-friendly ICT systems, the steps of communication and *user processing/understanding* might move closer together as users pull off information from the system themselves. Finally, this information is converted into *decisions* about what to do, and when to do it, with regard to promoting a group, and the information cycle ends up where it began, in the *'real world'*.

This is, of course, a highly simplified version of a complex and iterative process. The diagram ignores the human factors important to effective information management. But thinking about management information as a system can help us identify opportunities for improvement and development (not all involving vast investment in technology) which can make a significant difference to our success.

Whether you currently work from a card index or are outgrowing your current database facilities, developing a management information system requires extensive planning. You need to consider how your organisation is developing and its likely need for information in the future. How many supporters is it realistic to aim for? What uses would be made of a new system were your plans to indicate the need for one? What do you want it to do and what benefits would it bring? What other organisational changes does all this imply? What costs are likely to be involved? For example, once you start to depend on a computerised information system for your operations and income, you need to have a minimum number of staff able and willing to use it. Otherwise a combination of holidays and sickness can paralyse the organisation, with no one able to put information in or get it out. You will therefore have to make some decisions: whether it is sensible doing it yourself or contracting an agency; on the scale and sophistication of the system; on the hardware and software; on the consultants who will advise you. All this is likely to involve conflicting advice and views, both from within and outside your organisation!

Box 1.3 sets out the key steps and issues to think about when developing a management information system.

BOX 1.3

A QUICK GUIDE TO PLANNING YOUR DATABASE

Getting started

It may seem obvious, but before getting started on a database project you'll need to make sure that you've got the following things in place to ensure your organisation is ready to complete and implement a database plan:

Agreement at senior management or board level that the database (and its planning) is one of the priorities for the organisation.

Staff time allocated to the planning process. This includes time for someone to coordinate the planning process, collect information on the needs of those who will be using the database etc. and time for users to give their input into the planning process. The amount of time taken for planning is often underestimated – it will obviously vary depending on the complexity of the database, size of the organisation etc. It would be wise, however, to allocate around 40 hours at least for the database coordinator to collect and collate the necessary information.

Funding

Funding should be sufficient to cover:

- staff time to develop the database plan
- the cost of buying or building the database
- staff time to test the database (e.g. to test a range of off-the-shelf products or test the database throughout the development process)
- training staff to use the database
- staffing and managing the database.

Planning essentials

As part of the planning process you'll need to look at:

- the information you currently collect
- any information you might want to collect in future
- what reports you need to produce – the information you want to get out of the database (e.g. who uses your services broken down by ward, advice queries by type, membership status)
- how information flows through your organisation (how information is collected, entered and reported, and who in the organisation performs these functions)
- whether to develop a custom database or whether to use an existing product – if so which product best suits your needs.

What should your database plan include?

Your database plan should be written in plain language, avoiding technical jargon as much as possible. It's helpful to include the following sections:

- *Summary/introduction* – outlining your organisation's objectives, why you need a database, what you want to achieve with the database, what sort of database you already have, how a new/ modified database will help your organisation achieve its objectives.
- *How information flows through your agency* – what data you need to collect, importing existing data, reports needed, what functionality the database must have (e.g. number of records it needs to be able to hold, search capabilities, integration with accounts software.

- *Implementation plan* – timescale for implementing the database including staff roles and responsibilities, properly costed budget.

- *Hardware/Software needs assessment and purchasing plan* – identifying minimum hardware and software requirements needed to run the database. Will any upgrades be needed? How much will they cost?

- *Staff resources needed (internal and external)* – which staff will use the database? Who will maintain the database? Will an external consultant be used? Identify any existing staff with appropriate technical skills.

- *Training needs* – which staff need training? Who will provide training? What type of training? How will current and future staff be trained?

- *Which product* you will use or who will build the database for you.

- *Who will support the database* – in house or external? Will a developer or existing product be used? What after-sales support will be available?

Time spent on the planning process will save a lot of heartache and is essential to give a clear idea of the type of database your organisation needs, can afford and support.

(Source: http://www.icthubknowledgebase.org.uk/planningyourdatabase)

1.6 SUMMARY

Here is a summary of the main learning points from this session:

- Information is a valuable resource, as much as financial or human resources, and needs to be carefully managed.

- We can distinguish between 'raw' data and information. Information is data which has been made useful by being transformed in a way which allows it to communicate knowledge or meaning to its receiver.

- Information management needs to consider the flow of information into, around and out of an organisation. Its main focus is to consider the regularly required information that helps people and groups inside and outside an organisation to carry out their responsibilities.

- Decisions about information management in an organisation depend on:
  - stakeholder needs
  - management style
  - the urgency and complexity of the information
  - the sensitivity of the information (i.e. the impact that losses or inaccuracies in the information would have)
  - the need to keep a record

- – the geographical spread of the organisation
- – the available communication options.
- Environmental scanning is the continuous search for indicators of emerging threats and opportunities using a variety of information sources.
- Good quality information should be:
  - – relevant
  - – clear
  - – sufficiently accurate
  - – complete (as appropriate to the situation)
  - – trustworthy
  - – concise
  - – timely
  - – communicated to the right person
  - – communicated via the right channel
  - – cost-effective.
- Protecting information involves securing it against loss or inappropriate disclosure. Legal responsibility for the collation, security, accuracy and use of personal information in an organisation lies with a named data controller.
- A database is a set of consistently structured records which can be manipulated in order to search, select, count and compare.
- List brokers buy, sell and rent databases. Computer bureaux offer information services such as suppression (removing unwanted records from a database before use), profiling (categorising records on a database according to agreed variables such as demographics) and data enhancement (improving the quality or utility of a database by correcting errors or combining records with other information).
- Databases date rapidly and require continual maintenance and development.
- Prospect research is concerned with identifying individuals capable of providing substantial help to an organisation as donors or volunteers.
- A management information system integrates the strategic use of information to optimise decision making in an organisation. It can be defined as 'A system to convert data from internal and external sources into information, and to communicate that information, in an appropriate form, to managers at all levels in all functions to enable them to make timely and effective decisions for planning, directing and controlling the activities for which they are responsible' (Lucey, 1998, p. 14).

Session 2
Managing People

CONTENTS

2 MANAGING PEOPLE

2.1 INTRODUCTION

All fundraising activity requires people, so managing and motivating your team of volunteers and staff is a key skill for fundraising managers, yet is one of the most difficult aspects of management. We have all experienced times when the behaviour of other people at work seems unusual, difficult to explain, or even bizarre. We may know some individuals who are apparently thoroughly committed to their work despite being under great stress, and others who seem demotivated despite being very well paid. Equally volunteers and people on committees may not always do the things that they are asked to, and sometimes do some quite unexpected things! Managers have to understand the issues that lead people to respond differently to similar incentives or conditions of work.

You might try to explain these variations by arguing that individuals have different goals, drives, interests, experiences and values, and that these shape how they respond to particular conditions and situations. Explanations such as 'she was demotivated because her needs were not being met' and 'he was satisfied because his efforts were being rewarded' emerge. You might then argue that certain organisational factors influence behaviour. Organisations shape what we do, both directly through enforcing formal rules, and indirectly through socialisation. This suggests that behaviour cannot be explained by individual factors alone. Rather, it is a product of the interaction between individual and organisational factors; between individual needs and social conventions; between doing what is in our interest and doing what is allowed. An awareness of this balance is at the heart of managing people, whether paid or unpaid, and managers need to be sensitive to the way in which individual characteristics and organisational pressures simultaneously shape individual behaviour.

Aims and learning outcomes

This session will explore the issues involved in managing people in a fundraising context. The aims of the session are:

- to identify some key management skills in motivating and leading a fundraising team
- to examine team roles and what makes an effective team
- to consider approaches to setting team and individual goals and allocating tasks.

First, we will discuss some of the factors that motivate people at work, offering some theories of motivation, and will then explore the extent to which volunteer motivation differs from that of paid workers. Second, we will look at the complexities of working with groups and teams. Third, we will look at the issues involved in dividing up the work and allocating tasks.

After studying this session you should be able to:

- explain some of the key management skills in motivating and leading a fundraising team
- demonstrate how different team roles can contribute to effective team working
- apply what you have learned to the context of your own organisation, to setting team and individual goals, and allocating tasks
- evaluate your own experiences and professional approach to managing people.

2.2 GETTING THE BEST OUT OF PEOPLE

People produce their best work when their 'E' factors are released (Handy, 2004). These are *energy, excitement* and *enthusiasm*. Participative fundraising in particular can be great fun while also bringing in much needed cash, and we all know that doing something really enjoyable often feels like it isn't really work – when in fact it is. Raising money and securing resources successfully can leave us all basking in a warm glow of success, and this section explores how to support and motivate your staff and volunteers to release their energy and excitement.

One of the problems in dealing with people is that we often assume that their behaviour stems from rational economic motives. According to the rational economic model people are primarily motivated by economic self-interest. They will act to maximise their own *financial* and *material* rewards. This view is essentially the same as that underlying much economic theory. The model suggests that people's efforts can largely be controlled by offering or withholding financial rewards. The importance of how people feel about their work is ignored as irrelevant in this model. But this view is obviously flawed when we think about volunteers, as they are unpaid. Consider the case in Box 2.1.

BOX 2.1

CONFLICT AT THE CHARITY SHOP

Jane had trained as an assistant manager for a small chain of newsagents. She had recently left the job to become manager of a large charity shop. The shop had previously been managed by a volunteer but it had become too much for her. Jane was really enthusiastic about the new job; she believed in the cause of the charity and relished the opportunity to exercise the extra responsibility that the job gave her. The regional shops manager, who had a background as a manager in a top retail store, had given all the local managers a pep talk at their last staff meeting. The shops were not making as much money as they used to and it was up to them to get the shops running on a more commercial basis. Jane felt under enormous pressure to increase the turnover of the shop to justify her position. One of her first steps was to implement a change in the price structure of goods in the shop. She felt that prices were too low. This was done without consulting the volunteers in the shop, some of whom were very unhappy about this change. The previous manager had always discussed changes with them. They felt that the shop provided a service to local people and that the change in pricing was making the clothes too expensive for their customers. Three of the volunteers who were involved in grading donated goods began deliberately to downgrade goods that came in. This was one way they felt that they could keep the shop how it had been. Jane was surprised to find in the following months that turnover was not increasing in the way she had expected.

ACTIVITY 2.1

Consider the case from the volunteers' perspective. What were their apparent motivations for working in the charity shop?

How did Jane's and the regional shops manager's motives differ from theirs?

Jane seemed to be motivated by the goals of efficiency and raising as much money as possible for the charity. The volunteers, on the other hand, were motivated, at least in part, by the desire to provide a service to local people as well as to raise funds for the charity. They also expected to be consulted over decisions affecting the shop. As a result there was a hidden conflict over how the shop should be run.

2.2.1 Everyone is different

When someone's behaviour does not match our expectations and we get annoyed because they are not doing what we want them to, we are often making some false assumptions. Here are three common misapprehensions:

- that we should only consider objective facts
- that everyone works for the same goals and has the same values
- that some behaviour just does not make sense and can therefore be discounted.

While these assumptions may be questionable, many managers base much of their behaviour on precisely these principles and ideas. Often we simplify the circumstances in order to make any progress at all. If we tried to take every complexity into account, paralysis would result. However, when social relations go wrong, the cause can frequently be found, not in the way things have been done, but in these three underlying assumptions that have been made about the people involved.

First, when making and defending difficult decisions, such as not to let a particular volunteer chair the fundraising committee even though they have offered to, managers often argue that they 'only considered the objective facts'. However, the assumption that facts and events can only be viewed in one way is limiting. Possibly the worst thing you can do as a manager is to regard people as stupid and difficult simply because they do not see things as you do. A first step in expanding your own view of events is to recognise that other, perfectly valid, accounts exist. Exploring other people's views will provide a richer understanding of the situation, perhaps more complex and less straightforward, but also more informed and possibly more insightful. This does not mean you have to agree with, or even accommodate, their views in the decisions you have to take; it does mean that your decisions may be better.

A second common mistake relates to goals and values, and the extent to which they are understood and shared. In politics and religion, for example, most of us accept differences between people as a fact of life. However, when it comes to work, whether paid or unpaid, managers often fall into the trap of assuming that everyone is working towards the same goals, namely those of the organisation. Many management decisions take it for granted that the people who implement them will cooperate in order to achieve the collective goals. The real reasons why people cooperate often have nothing to do with achieving the collective goals and everything to do with achieving their own goals. Fortunately, in many cases the two are not incompatible. Indeed, it has been suggested that the art of effective people management is to ensure that personal, team and organisational goals match, so that all may be attained simultaneously. To achieve compatibility between personal and organisational goals, managers need to know something of the goals that people are seeking to attain through their work and some of the needs that push people to work willingly in difficult conditions. For example, the 'gift element' in volunteering is important and no one would deny the values that it represents. There are, however, implications in seeing volunteering *solely* in this way. It implies that you cannot turn a volunteer down; it does not give recipients much of a say in the relationship (they become indebted); and it ignores the fact that management and resources are still needed to support people who give their time for free. Thinking back to the 'gift–exchange continuum' that we introduced in Book 3, it is often more appropriate to think of volunteering as an *exchange* rather than a gift. It does not take away the giving element but it makes the relationship more equal: the volunteer offers the organisation what it needs, in return for receiving something from the organisation.

The third false assumption is that the behaviour of other people does not make sense. No matter how hard managers try to understand it, some people's behaviour just seems plain awkward or defies explanation, and the temptation therefore is to dismiss it. An example might be the volunteer who just will not stick to their own remit, but keeps interfering in tasks that have been allocated to others. However, in many instances the recognition that something does not make sense can be an important step in enhancing our understanding and knowledge of a particular situation. If things do not make sense to us it may mean that we are missing some information about events. Alternatively, it may tell us that we are lacking an appropriate understanding of the situation. We may not be sufficiently sensitive to the range of conventions and rules governing the events taking place. In the case of the volunteer, it may be that they would like a more responsible role but are not assertive enough to discuss this with you.

2.2.2 Some theories of motivation

There are many different theories of motivation. Some suggest that people work to meet different types of need. For example, Maslow (1954) developed the idea of a hierarchy of needs (see Figure 2.1). He suggested that there are five categories of need which apply to people in general, and which should be met if they are to develop a meaningful relationship with their work. Maslow's hierarchy, from a basic level upwards, is:

1 physiological needs – food, drink and shelter
2 security needs – protection against danger and threat
3 social needs – love, affection and acceptance as part of a social group
4 self-esteem needs – to have high self-esteem and the respect of others (prestige, status)
5 self-actualisation needs – to realise our potential and develop skills, to become what we believe we are capable of becoming.

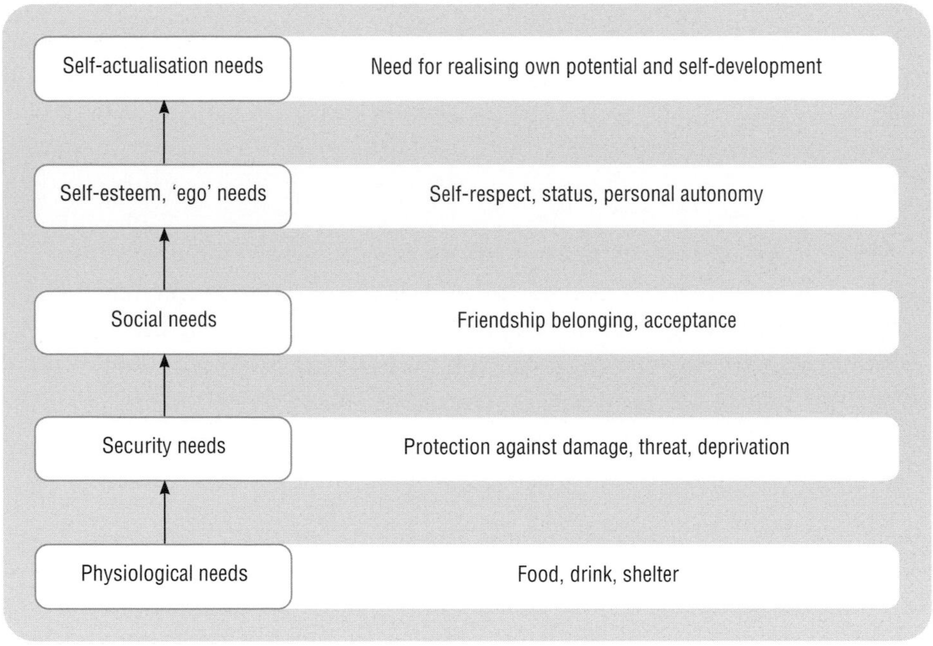

Self-actualisation needs	Need for realising own potential and self-development
Self-esteem, 'ego' needs	Self-respect, status, personal autonomy
Social needs	Friendship belonging, acceptance
Security needs	Protection against damage, threat, deprivation
Physiological needs	Food, drink, shelter

Figure 2.1   Maslow's hierarchy of needs

Certainly this seems to fit with some of the ideas about volunteer motivation outlined above. Table 2.1 illustrates some ways in which these needs may be met for volunteers and staff.

Table 2.1   Simple prescriptions based on a hierarchy of needs

These needs ...	can be met through ...
Physiological	Good working conditions, attractive wage, salary or expenses for participation (e.g. travel and childcare costs, subsidised housing, free or subsidised catering)
Security	Attractive pension provision, safe working conditions, 'no redundancy' policy, attention to 'risks' of volunteering, ensuring boundaries are kept
Social	Sports and social events, office parties, outings, permission for informal activities, encouraging open communications
Self-esteem	Regular positive feedback, prestige, job titles, photographs in news-sheets, promotions, clear volunteer job descriptions, supervision, training and support (including volunteers!), allowing responsibility to be taken by experienced and skilled volunteers, recognition of volunteers as part of the organisation
Self-actualisation	Challenging job assignments, discretion over core work activities, promotion opportunities, encouraging creativity, scope for volunteers to develop new skills and confidence in themselves, help to achieve their objectives such as new employment direction or a role in life post-retirement

(Source: Based on Huczynski and Buchanan, 2003)

ACTIVITY 2.2

(a) In terms of Maslow's hierarchy of needs, which of your needs are currently satisfied by your present occupation?

_____

_____

(b) Now think of a paid worker and a volunteer in a typical voluntary sector or non-profit organisation. Which needs do you think are being satisfied for each individual?

_____

_____

(c) Can you think of any shortcomings of Maslow's hierarchy of needs as an explanation of behaviour?

_____

_____

Probably most or all of the lower-level needs are satisfied for you, the staff member and the volunteer. But perhaps the volunteer, in particular, may be less able to satisfy his or her higher-level needs at work.

Maslow's theory is a broad generalisation about human behaviour. It does little to explain individual differences in behaviour. Why do some people seem to have a greater need for money or social esteem than others? Research studies have also cast doubt on the strict hierarchical ordering of needs.

Another way of looking at behaviour and motivation in organisations is as a *psychological contract*. This approach was developed by Edgar Schein (in Pugh, 1996) who argued that motivation was complex and different for different individuals even in similar contexts. Here motivation is an outcome of the relationship between an individual and the situation in which he or she works. This can be thought of in terms of a contract between the individual and the organisation he or she works for (see Figure 2.2).

The psychological contract is essentially a set of expectations. The individual has a set of outcomes or rewards that he or she expects from work, in return for which he or she expects to expend certain energies and talents in doing the work of the organisation. Similarly, the organisation has certain expectations of what it wants the individual to contribute to the work of the organisation, and certain rewards and outcomes that it will give the individual in return. The terms of the psychological contract are not stated

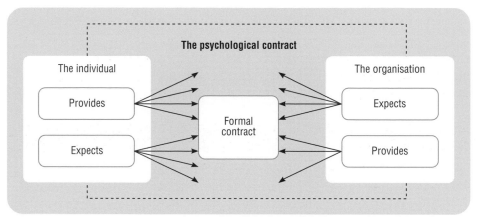

Figure 2.2 A diagrammatic representation of the psychological contract

explicitly, unlike in employment contracts and other formal agreements, and participants may remain unaware of what is expected of them. There are obvious parallels between the psychological contract an individual may have with an employer and the 'implicit' elements of any deal between two or more organisations.

Schein argues that managers should be good *diagnosticians* and value the *spirit of enquiry*. Those with responsibilities for managing people need to value *diversity* and be sensitive to people's differing circumstances and different cultural backgrounds. There are four important implications that stem from the idea of a psychological contract:

1   Most individuals are members of more than one organisation or group, and consequently have more than one psychological contract. They will not necessarily try to satisfy all their needs and goals within one contract. Thus motivations which might work very well in one situation might not be relevant to another because they are already being satisfied elsewhere.

2   A psychological contract which is not perceived similarly by both parties is likely to become a source of trouble or conflict. If the organisation expects more than the individual wishes to give, this may lead him or her to feel exploited, whereas the organisation may feel the individual lacks commitment or is lazy (see Box 2.2).

3   Efforts to improve motivation are likely to be effective only if both parties view the contract in similar ways.

4   People's and organisations' expectations change over time, hence the psychological contract will change. For example, someone who is young and single may be prepared to work long and irregular hours for better pay or promotion. When that person is older and has a family, he or she may put increased value on working more regular hours and having increased leisure time. Later in life, when they are retired, they may be looking for a different kind of commitment, maybe as a volunteer, that gives them status and a role that they used to get from their job.

The management implication of this approach to motivation is that it stresses the importance of people with fundraising management responsibilities reaching an agreement on the appropriate psychological contract with staff and volunteers, as otherwise problems are likely to arise (illustrated in Box 2.2).

BOX 2.2

MISMATCHING EXPECTATIONS

A volunteer agrees to attend fundraising subcommittee meetings regularly and to be the honorary secretary, taking the minutes. Her psychological contract includes – 'in the limited time I have this is the most useful way I can make a contribution; I'll be appreciated for this'. The staff see her interest in the committee as a basic commitment to the work of the organisation and seek to draw her in further. They invite her to help out at an exhibition by interviewing new volunteers, and to be part of a staff group looking at future fundraising strategy for the agency. The result is that the secretary feels put upon and mistreated; the staff feel that she is not really committed and involved. Just before a major fundraising event is due to happen the secretary announces that she will have to resign the post.

This negotiation of a psychological contract suggests a process where each side spells out its expectations of the other, and comes to some form of workable agreement. In reality this is often easier said than done. People are often not fully aware of their expectations, or they may find it difficult to express them. They may lack confidence or feel it is somehow not legitimate to talk about their expectations. You will need to be sensitive to signs that things are not quite right, such as individuals failing to turn up to committee meetings without apology. Perhaps there is frustration or dissatisfaction – you will need to probe carefully for the mismatch of expectations underlying these problems. Expectations will also change over time, as circumstances change, so a psychological contract that was balanced may become unbalanced. You will need to rediscover and review the nature of the contract as circumstances and expectations change.

ACTIVITY 2.3

Think of someone who works with you (paid or unpaid). List the three most important things you expect that person to put into her or his work, and what you think are the three most important rewards she or he experiences from this work. (You may find it easier first to list as many expectations and rewards as you can think of, and then to select the three most important ones.)

Expectations

1 _____

_____

2 _____

_____

3 _____

_____

Rewards

1 _____

_____

2 _____

_____

3 _____

_____

Now, if you can, ask this colleague what she or he thinks are the three most important things she or he expects to put into work and the three most important things she or he expects to get out of work.

Expectations

1 _____

_____

2 _____

_____

3 _____

_____

Rewards

1 _____

_____

2 _____

_____

3 _____

_____

Compare the two lists. Do your expectations coincide? If not, how do you think the psychological contract might be improved?

2.2.3 Is volunteer motivation 'different'?

Many voluntary and not-for-profit organisations rely heavily on voluntary labour – labour which is given freely and without payment. Much of the management research and literature on motivation has been on paid employees, and it is usually assumed that pay is an important incentive to work. This assumption does not apply to volunteers, so is their motivation different? The answer is both yes and no. There are both similarities with and differences from the motivations of employees, but fortunately the theories we have been discussing are applicable.

Understanding the motivations of volunteers is important. Volunteers are not dependent on the organisation they work for to meet their basic needs. They are not tied by a formal employment contract. As a result volunteers are usually freer than employees to pick and choose the organisation to which they give their time and efforts. In addition, if demographic changes or changes in the patterns of paid employment cause the pool of potential volunteers to shrink, then unless voluntary and not-for-profit organisations offer volunteers an appealing environment and motivating work, they are likely to experience problems in recruitment and retention.

Research suggests that the motivations of volunteers, like those of paid workers, are numerous and varied (see Box 2.3). So, beware of simplistic assumptions. People are too often assumed to volunteer for altruistic motives, the selfless desire to help others. While much research suggests that altruism is an important component of many people's motives, there is no evidence for pure altruism in which people's actions are utterly without some form of benefit to themselves. Voluntary work, like paid work, can meet many different needs and goals: challenging and interesting work and the chance to exercise some power and to influence events may meet growth needs; increased social contact may meet social needs. Through voluntary work people may be better able to pursue their wider interests and goals: to further their political ends, to campaign for social change, to work with others to help address a particular problem or disability that they have.

As with paid work, it would be foolish for management to look for, or rely on, universal generalisations about what motivates volunteers. Instead it is much better to follow the lessons of Schein's complex model of human nature and treat each person as potentially different with her or his own needs and expectations of voluntary work. Again this highlights the need to negotiate an appropriate psychological contract with each volunteer. In order to do this effectively it is important for organisations to be particularly clear about what they expect from volunteers and what rewards or incentives they can offer them. For example, one voluntary agency has a volunteer agreement which lists under headings, such as expenses and time, what the agency expects of the volunteer and what the volunteer can expect of the agency. Box 2.3 illustrates some of these issues.

BOX 2.3

A CHOICE BLEND

The crucial point about volunteering is that it is freely given and done without compulsion. Anything that abrogates the spirit of choice in volunteering endangers the willingness of people to go on doing it. What puts volunteers off is feeling used, not appreciated, not consulted and not accommodated. The full report of this research identifies the needs and actions associated with each pressure point to encourage positive feelings towards volunteering and enable the transition from non-volunteer to committed lifelong volunteer. There are, of course, resource implications because effective volunteer management needs people and systems in place to provide it. However, the pay-off is beyond dispute.

Volunteers want to feel welcome, secure, respected, informed, well-used and well-managed. Since they do not have the incentive of a pay packet, rewards must be supplied in other ways by the organisation. The task for volunteer management is to find the right blend: combining choice and control, flexibility and organisation, to be experienced by the volunteer as a blend of informality and efficiency, personal and professional support. This must take full account of the mix of characteristics, motivations and needs within the volunteer workforce, and the type of volunteering and context in which it is carried out. For the volunteering infrastructure as a whole, this suggests a blend of different management approaches and structural arrangements, rather than over-dependence on a single model.

(Source: Gaskin, 2003)

2.3 WORKING WITH GROUPS

Groups are an essential component of organisations. They are absolutely essential to most aspects of fundraising. They are used, among other things, to organise work, to coordinate different activities, to solve problems and to make decisions. People also naturally form themselves into informal groupings, for example, groups of friends and acquaintances. Most people who work in organisations spend a high proportion of their time in groups. It is important then that you understand something about how groups work and how you can function effectively in groups, whether as an 'ordinary' member of the group or in some special capacity such as a chair, leader or manager.

This section will look at types of groups and some of the problems you may experience in working with them.

2.3.1 Types of groups

Groups can have a powerful influence on human behaviour. When you join a group you are involved in a 'trade-off'. On the one hand there is a certain loss of freedom. You will be expected to abide by the rules of the group. Some of these rules may be explicit. For example, they may define who can be a member of the group, its purpose and the roles of key people in it. Many rules will be informal and might include modes of dress, what subjects can be talked about, how to address other members of the group and so on. In some groups, such as extreme political or religious groups, the social pressures to conform and the subsequent loss of individual freedom can be severe.

On the other hand, you will gain something from being a member of the group. There will be things that you can achieve as part of a group that you would not be able to achieve individually. People often use the word 'synergy' to refer to this kind of advantage of working with others.

There are various types of groups within organisations. Kakabadse et al. (1988, pp. 154–6) have suggested a useful categorisation: groups may be *formal* or *informal, primary* or *secondary* (see Figure 2.3).

	Formal	Informal
Primary	e.g. department, project team	e.g. group of friends
Secondary	e.g. large committee	e.g. a 'network' of black managers

Figure 2.3 Different types of groups

1 *Formal groups* – have some formal recognition and authority within the organisation and usually have some defined purpose or task related to the overall task of the organisation. They might be departments, work groups or project teams. An organisation can be regarded as consisting of an interlocking set of such work groups.

2 *Informal groups* – do not have formal authority, but can sometimes be more powerful than their formal counterparts, leading to difficulties in management. Individuals within organisations interact with a wide range of other people who may not be part of their formal groups. They may form relationships with those people to pursue common interests, or to make various exchanges. Informal groups may form to fulfil special needs and goals: for example, to provide friendship, a sense of identity and belonging, or to pursue a common interest such as a sport. They may also form to pursue work-related interests: for example, a group of women managers may meet to discuss common problems and provide mutual support.

3 *Primary groups* – are those whose members have regular and frequent interactions with each other, in the pursuit of some common interests or tasks. A small work group, project team or family are all primary groups. They usually have an important influence on their members' values, attitudes and beliefs.

4   *Secondary groups* – are those whose members interact less frequently. They are often larger than primary groups. A large committee, a professional group or an association are all examples. Their members do not have the opportunity to get to know each other well. As a result they are usually less cohesive than primary groups.

Formal groups are used for a variety of functions in organisations, which typically require different skills, knowledge, perspectives or interests to be brought together to carry them out.

Although informal groups by their very nature do not usually have clearly defined organisational purposes, they may in fact serve some of the functions outlined in the following list. For example, a group of staff members who meet regularly to play badminton may also serve as a channel for passing on information, or to discuss past events and problems.

Informal groups may be involved in:

*   distributing and managing work
*   problem solving and decision taking
*   passing on information
*   coordinating and liaising
*   enabling people to participate in decision making
*   negotiation or conflict resolution
*   inquest or enquiry into the past.

A common source of difficulties with groups is when the same group is expected simultaneously to perform two different functions. A management meeting, for example, which starts as a negotiation between departments is unlikely to proceed very satisfactorily to a discussion of the long-term plan of the organisation. Thus the functions of groups often need to be separated, perhaps by time, place or title, or by a change of style. For example, a committee might find it useful to separate the parts of meetings dealing with administrative matters from those dealing with future plans, and to adopt a different style for each part of the meeting. The committee may adopt a fairly brisk and formal style to deal with routine administration, and then have a break and choose a more relaxed and participative style to deal with future plans. It may want to take this further and have occasional review days off-site to discuss plans in more detail.

Individuals, too, may use groups to serve a variety of different needs and interests – some of the main ones are summarised in the following list.

*   satisfying social needs
*   establishing or confirming an identity
*   gaining help and support in carrying out their particular objectives (which may not be the same as the organisation's)
*   sharing and helping in a common activity.

ACTIVITY 2.4

Consider one formal and one informal group that you belong to at work or in a leisure context.

(a) Note down for each group what are the organisational uses and individual pay-offs.

	Organisational uses	Individual pay-offs
Formal group		
Informal group		

(b) How well do you feel that each group manages to perform its task(s) and meet individual social needs?

Formal group

Informal group

2.3.2 Group development

Like individuals, groups mature and develop. Research suggests that groups go through various common stages of development. The effectiveness of the group will depend in part on how well it deals with the distinctive problems that emerge at each of these stages of development. One of the best known and most useful models of group development has been proposed by Tuckman (1965). He suggests that groups go through four stages: 'forming', 'storming', 'norming' and 'performing', which can be summarised as follows.

1 *Forming* – At this stage the group is not fully a group but rather a collection of individuals. It is characterised by general talk about the purpose, identity, composition, life-span, leadership and working arrangements of the group. Individuals are usually keen to make an impression on the group and establish their own personal identities.

2 *Storming* – Most groups go through a period of conflict after an initial superficial consensus. At this stage, the purpose, leadership and other roles, working patterns and behaviour of the group or of its members may all be challenged. People's individual goals, or 'personal agendas', may be revealed during this process and some interpersonal conflict is to be expected. This stage is particularly important in the formation of trust within the group – people are testing out each other and the group, and revealing more about themselves. If successfully

handled this stage leads to the formulation of more realistic goals and procedures.

3   *Norming* – This stage is characterised by the group establishing the norms and patterns of work under which it will operate: for example, how it should work, how decisions are taken, what degree of openness, trust and confidence are appropriate between members. There will probably be much tentative experimentation by people who are testing feelings and opinions within the group and establishing their level of commitment.

4   *Performing* – Only when the previous three stages have been completed will the group be fully productive. Although some level of performance will have been achieved during earlier phases, output will have been diminished by the energy put into resolving the group processes and exploring individual objectives and roles. In many committees and groups which meet infrequently the basic issues of objectives, procedures and appropriate leadership patterns are never fully resolved, and may continue to hinder the group, often leading to frustration and reduced effectiveness.

More recent thinking suggests that a fifth and a sixth stage should be added – *adjourning* and *mourning*. This recognises that groups and teams often disband or re-form into other groupings once a task has been completed and it is necessary to recognise the characteristics of these stages as well. People may be feeling uncertain about the future and unhappy at the loss of the good relationships they had in their previous group. They may be experiencing stress in the transition from one group setting to another, in parting from the group or in having nothing specific to move on to. Managers can help here by giving supportive feedback on past performance and by encouraging people to continue networking with former colleagues in the group. Social events to mark the end of the work of a group are valuable too, not only as a way of marking the transition, but in interpersonal terms as well. If your group is intended to have a limited life-span, it may be as well to flag that at the outset, first so that people know what to expect, and second because very busy people may be persuaded to join who would not otherwise do so, safe in the knowledge that they know what time commitment is expected.

The time and effort needed to go through the stages of development will depend on the circumstances facing the group. For example, when the task is clearly defined and regarded by everyone as important, and the individuals are highly committed to the group and are used to working with each other, then the stages of development may be dealt with quite quickly. However, for many new groups these conditions do not hold and they will take time to work through the stages. In particular it is important to accept and work through the storming stage. In some cultures overt conflict is regarded as unacceptable behaviour and this can mean that open disagreement and hostility in groups are repressed, but this can have a cost in the quality of their outputs.

It is also worth remembering that, when someone leaves or joins a group, it becomes a new group, and so the process of group development will be repeated. For example, if an influential member of the group leaves there will probably be renewed jockeying for influence and position in the group.

Tuckman's theory has two key implications:

1 A degree of conflict, disagreement and jockeying for position is to be expected early on in the life of a group, or when its composition changes.

2 A group will need some time to develop before it can work at full effectiveness; ideally this should be allowed for in plans for the group.

This means that groups do not always work smoothly and often you sense this without really understanding why this is. Tuckman's theory should help you to understand why that key planning meeting of the joint liaison group did not go as well as you hoped. However, there are several other problems which confront groups. Four will be discussed here: *hidden agendas, blind spots, group anxiety* and *'groupthink'*.

2.3.3 Some common problems

Hidden agendas and blind spots

In attempting to understand group dynamics it is important to recognise that levels of self-awareness between members of a group will differ. An individual will be aware of things that other members of the group are not aware of and vice versa. As we saw earlier, individuals bring their own objectives to groups. Things that an individual wants or expects from the group that the group does not know about are called *hidden agendas*.

Common examples of hidden agendas are:

• someone using a meeting to impress another colleague

• someone resisting a proposal on spurious grounds because he or she is not prepared to reveal the real reasons, for example, they may see you as trying to get a share of 'their' budget

• someone using a meeting to embarrass or 'put down' another member of the group for his or her own personal reasons.

The best way to handle hidden agendas is often to bring them into the open early on – at the storming stage of group development. For example, the group might have a round robin on 'What are we personally hoping for from this project?' or 'What are our departments hoping to get out of this working party?'

Of course, there is no guarantee that people will be open about their motives. It may be that they bring issues and prejudices to the workplace of which they themselves are barely aware. However, if you are prepared to be open about your agendas, particularly if you occupy a position of authority, others are more likely to be open about theirs – and then the group has far more of the information it needs to be effective. Resolving the differences may still be difficult, but at least everyone understands the situation and the group is likely to waste less time prevaricating.

The second type of inequality of self-awareness, when other group members know things about an individual that the individual does not know, is *blind spots*. A typical example of a blind spot is where the group is unwilling to tell someone that the real reason why her or his offer of help is not being accepted is because no one believes that she or he can do it. This can be a common problem for fundraisers working with volunteers who may aspire to undertake tasks that are beyond their capabilities.

One of the main reasons for blind spots is that the group members are afraid of hurting the feelings of another group member. It is never easy to tell people that you do not feel that they are competent, or that you do not trust them. However, while blind spots remain the individual concerned is clearly disadvantaged. He or she can do nothing to challenge the assumptions of the rest of the group, or try to change his or her own behaviour. Again the best remedy is usually to try sensitively to bring the situation out into the open. It may be better for a member of the group to tell the individual about the group's feeling in private, to reduce the chances of public humiliation and to give the person a chance to collect his or her thoughts before having to deal with the whole group.

As these examples show, both hidden agendas and blind spots can damage the effectiveness of groups. Increasing a group's level of openness and self-awareness of these problems can increase trust and release energy.

Group anxiety

Group relationships are on the whole more stressful than individual relationships and, generally, the larger the group, the greater the stress. People tend to feel exposed, on show and uncertain of where they fit in, particularly certain types of volunteer who may lack confidence through having been ill or unemployed for some time. This can also apply when there is a dominant individual who may not be sensitive to the fact that others are less confident. This is particularly true in new groups and at large formal gatherings and meetings, where there is less opportunity for immediate confirmation and feedback from other people and more space for fantasies to grow about what other people think or intend.

The anxiety this causes can be coped with creatively or destructively, both collectively by the group and by individuals. Collectively, the group may develop norms and structures that will alleviate anxiety and create a good working environment. Individually, people may develop communication skills and personal sensitivity that will reduce the element of fantasy in the group and promote personal contact. Alternatively, individuals may be left to cope in their own characteristic and idiosyncratic ways with whatever anxiety they feel.

People may:

- talk too much through embarrassment
- intellectualise to get away from their anxious feelings
- chat to a neighbour to get some personal contact
- be so worried that they cannot listen and then ask irrelevant questions
- turn up late because they are worried about coming at all, or as a form of silent protest
- make bad jokes at inopportune moments
- attack and criticise others because they are afraid of being attacked themselves
- stray from the point because they are too anxious to concentrate
- smooth over all difficulties, try to keep things 'nice' and avoid confrontation
- continually apologise for themselves.

More seriously, people may:

- withdraw, hide, try to become inconspicuous
- look for someone stronger to protect them, ally themselves with the person most likely to win, regardless of the ally's views
- look for someone to attack and begin hostilities against the nearest likely victim – this often leads to *scapegoating* (the situation where one person, often a 'weaker' member of the group or its leader, is unreasonably and unfairly blamed for a group's difficulties) – the group fantasises that, if this person is excluded, all its problems will disappear.

It is common for people to feel anxious about:

- belonging and fitting in
- their value to the group
- how criticism and conflict will be dealt with.

One of the very important maintenance functions of a group is to ensure that these sources of group anxiety are dealt with in a way that is felt to be constructive and mutually acceptable.

ACTIVITY 2.5

Think of a group which you belong to (perhaps a fundraising committee).

Does the group have a clear, established way of dealing with the following events and issues, and how effective are they?

(a) Newcomers. How are they involved and helped to feel part of the group?

_____

_____

(b) Contributing to the group. In what ways are people encouraged to contribute to the group? How are people shown that their contribution is valued?

_____

_____

(c) Feedback and criticism. What are the accepted ways of:
- expressing appreciation?

_____

_____

- reviewing people's contributions to the meeting?

_____

_____

- expressing concern or dissatisfaction with people's actions or behaviour?

_____

_____

If there are no clear norms or if the established norms are ineffective or inappropriate, what changes would you like to see?

_____

_____

_____

_____

Not having clear, acceptable or effective ways of dealing with newcomers, conflict and criticism indicates anxiety within a group.

The following are some suggestions for how a group might begin to deal with these issues.

(a) The group leader must try to introduce newcomers to the group and make them feel welcome. Newcomers might be teamed up with more established members of the group while they settle in. Furthermore, the addition of a new member can set a group back a stage or two in Tuckman's sequence, creating 'storms' which need to be navigated.

(b) An important maintenance function in the group is to involve all members positively in the discussion. This is often a role taken on by the chair or coordinator of a group. Techniques such as round robins, buzz groups and brainstorming can also be used to encourage contributions. Listening carefully to and respecting someone's ideas is probably the most important way of valuing her or his contributions.

(c) Feedback and criticism are more likely to be accepted and acted on if they are constructive, that is, aimed at improving behaviour rather than concerned with blaming or sanctioning someone. Positive feedback is important in maintaining motivation and morale – simply thanking people for their efforts is very effective. Thinking about how and when you give feedback is really important.

You may well have thought of other things that could reduce group anxiety and improve effectiveness.

Groupthink

Groupthink is the process whereby a group ignores evidence which might suggest that what it is planning to do, or has done, is ill-advised. The term was originally coined by Janis (1972) after his study of several disastrous decisions made by the United States presidency, including the invasion of North Korea and the 'Bay of Pigs' in Cuba. In each case, warnings sounded about the dangers were ignored. Janis suggested that under certain conditions commitment to the group overrides the ability to assess situations realistically. These conditions are:

- the group faces a situation where an important decision has to be made, under severe time pressure
- the group is already fairly cohesive
- the group has a tendency to isolate itself from outsiders
- the leader has a preferred solution which the group actively pursues.

It is important for groups, especially those that are close-knit, to realise that they are liable to groupthink, which can be recognised by the following symptoms:

- an exaggerated sense of the group's importance and a feeling of invulnerability
- unanimity
- the rationalising away of less-preferred options
- appeals to morality
- stereotyping of opponents in negative terms
- pressure on members to conform
- self-censorship of doubts.

There are several possible defences against groupthink:

First, try to ensure that important groups contain people with some diversity of opinions;

Second, try to aim for a moderate rather than a high degree of consensus in the group. If there is a high degree of consensus then invite one or two people to play the role of devil's advocate.

Alternatively, new members with different ideas could be invited into the group, the disadvantage being that the group would need to re-form, which of course takes time.

Groupthink and scapegoating are processes by which members often resist making changes to the group and how it works. Groups resist changes for many of the reasons that individuals do – they have their own vested interests to protect, to admit that they are wrong may cause members pain and discomfort, and so on. We now turn to some of the issues you may encounter in working with teams of people on fundraising issues.

2.4 WORKING WITH TEAMS

Teams are special kinds of groups with the following characteristics:

- a common goal or task to pursue
- the pursuit of this goal or task requires collaboration and the coordination of activities among the team's members
- the team members have regular and frequent interactions with each other.

It is often assumed that there is a high degree of equality between members of teams, but this is not always the case. Teams may be established for different reasons and take on a variety of forms. Teams are frequently established to tackle particular discrete *tasks*. For example, one local environmental group, consisting largely of volunteers and with a small paid staff, set up a project group to raise funds for a major fundraising initiative. A range of tasks was identified including research, letter writing, producing a newsletter, holding public meetings and staging exhibitions. Small teams of three to eight people were established to tackle each of the tasks with the help of a coordinating group. The teams were short-term and were dissolved once they had completed their tasks. They had the advantage of involving several people in work that was new to them, while at the same time using the experience of those who had particular experience.

Small task teams are frequently established to develop new strategies or policies in a particular area and are often called *working parties* or *working groups*.

Sometimes teams are established around a particular *function*. For example, the administrative group in an organisation may become an administrative team, or fundraisers may form a fundraising team. *Location* is another basis on which teams develop. Close collaboration and coordination of work can occur between people sharing the same location. This is quite common where a national organisation has several small offices or field bases in different parts of the country. However, collaboration and coordination can also occur where people just happen to work in the same room or part of a building, where there is a shared goal or task.

Teams are also commonly formed to undertake particular *projects*. Project teams are normally established for a specific time and have

Our images of teams are so positive that the word 'team' is often used to describe any arrangement where staff are nominally grouped together, irrespective of whether they actually work together as a team. In fact, groups that do not work collaboratively may be called teams perhaps to hide this fact, or in the hope that greater collaboration will result.

a defined task or target to achieve. Quite often voluntary and not-for-profit projects are externally funded, and some staff may only be employed for the duration of the project. Project teams are usually distinguished from task teams by being longer term and having at least some workers who commit a high proportion or all of their working time to the project. Project teams also often have a higher degree of autonomy from the work of the rest of the organisation.

Working in teams has advantages, for example:

- the chance to bring together a variety of skills and experiences to tackle a problem or task
- the opportunity for people to learn from each other
- mutual support
- the potential for team members to enthuse and motivate each other
- a degree of independence from the rest of the organisation.

Team working may also have disadvantages, even when the team is working well, for example:

- too much isolation from the rest of the organisation, leading to goals being out of tune with organisational goals
- team pressures, leading to an unrealistic view of the world (groupthink)
- competition between teams, leading to conflict.

Of course, if the team is not working well, there may also be other disadvantages.

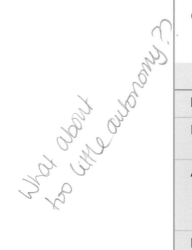

ACTIVITY 2.6

Think of two work teams of which you are, or have been, a member. For each team answer the following questions.

(a) What is each team called?

(b) What is the main purpose or function of each team?

(c) What would you say were the main advantages or disadvantages of working in each team?

	Team 1	Team 2
Name		
Purpose/function		
Advantages		
Disadvantages		

Some advantages which you might have mentioned include: bringing complementary skills to the task; mutual support; learning from each other; providing a degree of autonomy.

Some disadvantages which you might have mentioned include: the problem of groupthink; too much autonomy from the rest of the organisation; competition between teams leading to conflict.

2.4.1 Team roles

Effective teams have members who between them can perform certain key roles within the team. A study of management teams conducted by Belbin (1996) concluded that an effective team included the roles described in Table 2.2 and that every person has a preferred role or set of roles.

Too many people preferring one type of role in a team means a lack of balance; too few roles and some tasks do not get done. One person may perform more than one role, particularly in small teams. Equally, more than one person may contribute to a particular role.

What are the practical implications of Belbin's work? An initial reaction might be that we ought to select team members so that all the necessary roles are filled. Unfortunately this is usually not practical. Team membership is often largely predetermined by other factors, usually people's technical function or position, or we may be unaware of the roles people are good at performing. So how can Belbin's findings be used in fundraising?

The first step is to develop an understanding of people's role preferences. You do not need elaborate psychometric tests for this. Conclusions can be drawn from observing how people behave in teams, and discussing with them their preferences. Some people will have strong preferences for one or two roles; others will be more flexible and be capable of filling several roles. Many fundraisers prefer the 'resource investigator' role, but too many team members with this preference may mean a great deal of competition between members and/or that nothing gets done. Your understanding can be used in two ways.

1 People are likely to be more effective if the tasks they are given allow them to operate in their preferred roles. For example, the 'implementer' should be allowed to do the administrative and scheduling tasks for the team.

2 Identifying people's preferred roles in a team can allow important gaps to be identified. It may be possible to fill a gap by importing a new person into the team, or perhaps more commonly by persuading a more 'flexible' member of the team to take on a new role.

Talk about limelight project group.

Implicit in Belbin's findings is the idea that one person does not have to provide all the leadership within a team. Different people can play different leadership roles.

Belbin® Team-Role Summary Descrptions

Team-Role Descriptions

Team Role	Contribution	Allowable Weakness
Plant	Creative, imaginative, unorthodox. Solves difficult problems.	Ignores incidentals. Too pre-occupied to communicate effectively.
Resource Investigator	Extrovert, enthusiastic, communicative. Explores opportunities. Develops contacts.	Over-optimistic. Loses interest once initial enthusiasm has passed.
Co-ordinator	Mature, confident, a good chairperson. Clarifies goals, promotes decision-making, delegates well.	Can be seen as manipulative. Offloads personal work.
Shaper	Challenging, dynamic, thrives on pressure. The drive and courage to overcome obstacles.	Prone to provocation. Offends people's feelings.
Monitor Evaluator	Sober, strategic and discerning. Sees all options. Judges accurately.	Lacks drive and ability to inspire others.
Teamworker	Co-operative, mild, perceptive and diplomatic. Listens, builds, averts friction.	Indecisive in crunch situations.
Implementer	Disciplined, reliable, conservative and efficient. Turns ideas into practical actions.	Somewhat inflexible. Slow to respond to new possibilities.
Completer Finisher	Painstaking, conscientious, anxious. Searches out errors and omissions. Delivers on time.	Inclined to worry unduly. Reluctant to delegate.
Specialist	Single-minded, self-starting, dedicated. Provides knowledge and skills in rare supply.	Contributes on only a narrow front. Dwells on technicalities.

ACTIVITY 2.7

This activity will help you review the performance of a team with which you are familiar. Choose a team which you belong to and whose performance you would like to review. Identify which colleagues in the team best fulfil the roles described by Belbin.

Role	Team member's name
Coordinator	
Shaper	
Plant	
Monitor/evaluator	
Resource investigater	
Implementor	
Team worker	
Completer/finisher	
Specialist	

(a) Which role (or roles) do you normally fill?

_____

_____

(b) Which roles come most easily to you, and which do you find most difficult?

_____

_____

(c) Are there any significant gaps in the composition of your team?

_____

_____

(d) If so, how do you think this affects the functioning of the team?

_____

_____

_____

(e) What do you think you could do about the gaps in your team?

_____

_____

2.4.2 Clarifying individual goals and allocating tasks

A team is more likely to be effective if it has a goal that is clear and that team members feel is important and worthwhile. This is more likely if they can participate in the formulation of the goal and how it is to be achieved. However, the views of the team will need to be balanced against wider organisational needs and expectations. In a long-serving team, or in one where there is a turnover of members, team goals will often need to be repeated and reinforced.

Once the team's overall goals are established, there is still the job of deciding the goals and priorities of individual team members and of allocating tasks to them. This will usually be done, at least partly, through joint discussion and negotiation within the team. The psychological contract, which we discussed earlier, can be helpful here in agreeing objectives. If the team has a manager, it will be the manager's responsibility to see that this is done effectively and provide regular supervision and appraisal.

There are three important considerations that the team and/or manager will need to bear in mind when allocating tasks and responsibilities:

- how well the task fits with the person's preferred role(s)
- who has the skills and experience to handle the task competently and efficiently
- who will find the task useful for their development.

How to strike the right balance between these often conflicting considerations will depend on the circumstances. If the task is very important or urgent it will probably be given to a skilled and experienced member of the team. In other circumstances the balance may tip in favour of the person who would benefit most from doing the task. Another way of trying to strike a balance is to give the task to two people, so that one person is learning from another.

Two of the most frequent excuses that managers give for not delegating tasks are that there is no one competent for them to delegate to, and that it is quicker to do the job themselves. While this failure to delegate may save time in the short-run, in the long-run it will probably lead to managerial overload and may undermine confidence and trust within the team – not to mention making an organisation look less credible to donors and funders.

Assuming that people have the adequate training and support, sharing tasks within the team is likely to encourage people to learn new skills, increase confidence and motivation, and reinforce trust.

2.5 SUMMARY

Here is a summary of the main learning points from this session:

- Handy (2004) points to the 'E' factors (energy, excitement and enthusiasm) as key to successful working.

- Three common misapprehensions about people-management problems are that there is only one 'objective' way of seeing things, that everyone shares the same goals and values, and that behaviour which you don't understand can be dismissed as meaningless.

- Maslow (1954) sees motivation in terms of satisfying a hierarchy of needs – from physiological, through security, social and self-esteem to self-actualisation needs.

- Schein (1996) describes the psychological contract, a set of unstated mutual expectations between an individual and an organisation. It has four implications for managing people:

  - most people have more than one psychological contract, which satisfy different needs

  - a psychological contract which is not understood in the same way by both parties creates potential conflict

  - effective motivation is only likely if both parties are brought to see the psychological contract in similar ways

  - the psychological contract (like the expectations which underpin it) changes over time. Managers thus need to be good diagnosticians and value a spirit of enquiry.

- Motivational theories apply to both paid and voluntary workers.

- Group membership involves a trade-off between individual autonomy and the power conferred by working with others.

- Kakabadse (1988) categorises groups as formal or informal, primary and secondary. Formal groups, such as project teams, have authority and status. Informal groups, such as friendship groups, lack formal authority but offer benefits such as mutual support. Primary groups, such as a family or project team, feature regular or frequent interactions. Secondary groups enjoy less frequent interactions and are often larger than primary groups. Examples include a large committee or a professional association.

- A common source of problems with groups is when they are required to perform two different functions at the same time.

- Tuckman (1965) describes group development through stages of forming, storming, norming and performing. Later theorists have added adjourning and mourning. The implication is that some conflict in group development is inevitable, and that groups take time to become effective.

- Common problems with groups include:

  - hidden agendas (things that an individual wants or expects from a group that its members are unaware of)

  - blind spots (when other group members know something about an individual that she or he does not know)

- group anxiety (e.g. the stress caused by exposure to the judgement of others in a group)
    - groupthink (Janis, 1972) (when a group ignores evidence which challenges its plans or thinking).
- Teams are groups with the following special characteristics:
    - a common goal or task
    - collaboration and coordination
    - regular and frequent interactions.
- Teams have the advantages of uniting skills and experience, creating mutual learning and support between members, and a degree of independence. They have the potential disadvantages of isolation from the larger organisation, groupthink and conflict between rival teams.
- Belbin (1996) argues that an effective team needs to include the roles of: coordinator, shaper, plant, monitor/evaluator, resource investigator, implementer, team worker, completer/finisher and specialist. Team members are more likely to be effective if they operate within their preferred role(s), and identifying such roles can allow important gaps to be filled by importing new members as appropriate.
- Effective teams have clear goals which their members feel are important and worthwhile. When allocating tasks within a team attention should be paid to members' preferred role(s), the skills and experience available from members, and the potential the task holds for individual development.

Managing Finance and Financial Performance

CONTENTS

3 MANAGING FINANCE AND FINANCIAL PERFORMANCE

3.1 INTRODUCTION

All fundraising involves funds – and that means handling figures. Whether planning a fundraising event, analysing the results of different activities, or showing how the resources you seek will be deployed to achieve your organisation's mission, you need to prepare and use figures to inform your decisions and support your case. What's more, fundraising competence means being comfortable and confident in handling those figures.

This session sets out the central concepts of financial management in fundraising contexts. Many of these ideas will be familiar to you already in other contexts, they are not actually difficult, and they will provide you with the reference points you need around which you can gradually develop your own understanding, familiarity and confidence.

Aims and learning outcomes

This session aims to:

- ensure familiarity with the basics of *costing*, *cash flow* and *budget management*
- highlight the significance of *overhead cost recovery* in preparing external bids, and the different ways it may be approached
- consider *evaluation and review* as they apply to financial management in fundraising
- introduce the concept of *benchmarking* and explore its uses (and abuses) in the context of fundraising.

After studying this session you should be able to:

- construct and use costings for activities for which you are responsible
- recognise when cash management may be an issue, and construct and use simple cash-flow forecasts
- anticipate the indirect and overhead costs likely to be generated by proposed activities
- join in discussions about overhead allocation and recovery in external bids, suggesting and defending principles you consider appropriate to your context
- suggest measures of financial performance appropriate to the fundraising activities you are involved in, explaining also their limitations and potential for misuse
- appraise, for the fundraising for which you and your organisation are engaged, the possible uses, costs, pitfalls and benefits of the main forms of benchmarking (external comparison)

- explain to colleagues the significance, and possible implications for your organisation, of externally compiled public comparisons of fundraising costs.

3.2 COSTING FOR BUDGETS AND CASH MANAGEMENT

This section sketches out the basic principles underpinning the two main techniques used for financial planning: *costing* and *cash-flow forecasting*. The aim is to show what these practices involve and to explain why they are an integral part of planning fundraising activities and events. The basic principles are illustrated by a very simple example.

3.2.1 Costing

The staff and friends of the hospice are planning their annual fête. They want it to be bigger and better than ever, involving as many people in the area as possible and raising a substantial amount of money in the process.

Someone suggests running a hamburger stall. Will it be worth the effort? After all, the hospice could probably sell the concession for the event to a little hamburger van for £50 and avoid all the trouble of organising it.

On the other hand, with upwards of 2,000 people expected, if half of them bought a hamburger at, say, 75p, that would be an income of at least £750 ... which sounds rather interesting ... but how much of that would be profit? To answer that question an estimate of the costs involved is needed. This is shown in Table 3.1.

Table 3.1 Hospice costing		
Item	**Details**	**Cost, £**
Bread	1,000 buns @ 7p	70
Meat	1,000 burgers @ 30p	300
Onions	Say 50 grams per burger, or 1,000 burgers = 50kg	
	50kg @ 70p per kilo	35
Gas	say	10
Cooking oil	guess	2
Cookers	hire for, say	20
Sauce and mustard	say	10
Serviettes	1000, say	15
		462

So a profit of £250 or more might be possible. Nevertheless, it is not obviously worthwhile: the members of staff cannot spend much of their time looking after the stall – they will have so much else to attend to. And then there is the question of the weather. What if it rains and they are left with 800 unsold burgers and buns? But the staff members agree that it would be worthwhile if they can hand over the running of the stall to some other group (such as a local youth group), providing they take care to minimise the risks.

Two weeks later a local youth club that is keen to run the stall has been found – this is great because it involves more people in the event. An agreement is reached on the understanding that any profit over £200 goes to the youth club, which considers that an increased price of 80p per hamburger is still reasonable to charge. After asking possible suppliers, a revised costing, which is now in effect a budget for the operation, is produced. See Table 3.2.

Table 3.2	Youth club costing	
Item	**Details**	**Cost, £**
Bread	1,000 buns @ 9p	90
Meat	1,000 50g burgers @ 20p	200
Onions	40kg @ 75p	30
Sauce and mustard		12
Cooking oil		2
Gas	cookers borrowed	12
Tables		12
Serviettes		10
Petrol	collection, delivery, etc.	7
		375

More significantly, the youth club will not place firm orders for the bread and meat until it has a weather forecast. In addition, the youth club reckons that if things are going well someone can be sent to the freezer centre to buy extra burgers and buns; so the youth club will be cautious with its initial order.

This simple task illustrates the following basic points about doing and using costings:

- Costing is essentially a commonsense procedure with which we are all familiar; for example, planning a holiday. It involves identifying all the different items, estimating (or finding out) how much they will cost and adding them up. Costing only becomes complicated if the activities being costed are complicated – or unfamiliar and uncertain.

- Costings are important in deciding whether a particular project or activity is worthwhile. A short-term financial assessment may not be the only consideration in fundraising – the fact that the hamburger stall was a way of cultivating a link with a local youth club was important in this case – but it would be unthinkable to proceed without considering costs.

- Like other planning techniques, costings can be done with different degrees of care and detail. Initially, a 'quick and dirty' exercise may be sufficient to show that an idea is worth pursuing; later, fuller and more reliable figures are needed before firm decisions are made.

- Costing helps in designing activities, in deciding how best to do them. It is clear from the costing which are the key items to attend to – in this example, the burgers and buns. If good prices can be obtained for them it will make a difference to the profits earned. Likewise, the financial implications of different ways of doing things and different levels of sales can be explored. In this case, the youth club wanted to avoid having unsold buns and burgers at the end of the day, while still wanting to sell as many burgers as possible. By trying out different assumptions and developing a contingency plan, they used the figures to help balance the risks and make the maximum safe profit for the effort being put into the exercise.

'Spreadsheet' computer programs make it easy to try out different assumptions and ask 'What if ...?' questions. All you have to do is modify the relevant figures and the computer immediately recalculates the totals.

- The costing provides the basis for a *budget* for the stall and allows a target to be set for those involved. When it comes to implementing the plan the youth club members can monitor the costs (in case, for example, mistakes have been made and the price needs to be adjusted) and as the day progresses they could, without too much difficulty, calculate how well they are progressing towards earning £200 for the hospice and £100 for the club.

3.2.2 Timing and the idea of cash flow

However, the preceding discussion has overlooked one point: the burgers, buns and so on had to be bought and paid for before the hamburgers were sold. So where did the money come from? Either the local suppliers have to provide credit, or the hospice or youth club need to have some cash available to cover the day or two between the expenses flowing out and the income flowing in. More generally, the problem is this: it is not enough to know that your income (from grants, membership fees, gift sales, shops, events, or whatever) will meet or exceed your outgoings. You also have to know *when* the money will arrive, and *when* you will have to make the payments. Otherwise you may find yourself unable to pay the wages or the electricity bill – because, for example, gift sales are concentrated over the Christmas period, but some major expenses will fall due in the autumn.

Table 3.3 shows one way of presenting a (simplified) cash-flow forecast – for a new community organisation that is seeking a grant of £72,000 to provide a community conciliation service. After some initial set-up costs, the main expenses are very predictable – staffing and office costs. The foundation from whom they are seeking funds usually pays its annual grant quarterly, in arrears. It looks like the organisation will have to borrow money – and of course the interest charged on that would be an additional cost. Alternatively, the community organisation might be able to use these figures to persuade the foundation to pay quarterly in advance ... that might be enough to prevent the need to borrow. Ah! – but would it? You can work this out for yourself: by changing the figures so that the grant income arrives in April, July, October and January.

Table 3.3 Granton Community Conciliation Service – cash-flow forecast April to March

(Grant received quarterly in arrears £000s)

	Apr	May	Jun	Jul	Aug	Sept	Oct	Nov	Dec	Jan	Feb	Mar	Year total
Income	0	0	18	0	0	18	0	0	18	0	0	18	72
Less expenditure	8.75	5.75	5.75	5.75	5.75	5.75	5.75	5.75	5.75	5.75	5.75	5.75	72
Plus carried forward from previous month	–	(8.75)	(14.5)	(2.25)	(8.00)	(13.75)	(1.5)	(7.25)	(13)	(0.75)	(6.5)	(12.25)	–
Monthly cash balance	(8.75)	(14.5)	(2.25)	(8.00)	(13.75)	(1.5)	(7.25)	(13)	(0.75)	(6.50)	(12.25)	0	0

Often, happily, cash flow may not be an issue for fundraisers – since they are generating a cash surplus from a steady series of activities they can, in effect, use some of what has been earned in earlier activities to meet any early expenses for the next round. Nevertheless, at times cash flow can be a very important consideration – for example, if you are starting up a fundraising department, embarking on a major capital appeal for which careful prospect research is essential, or simply introducing a new line of fundraising activity. In such cases you may necessarily incur considerable costs before the income starts to flow. If you are seeking financial support from a trust, public authority or bank they would often expect to see a cash-flow forecast. Indeed, it is good practice to consider how the grant will actually be paid (e.g. in arrears or with a certain percentage withheld until the final report is submitted etc.) as this might be a consideration your organisation would want to take into account before deciding to go ahead with the bid.

3.2.3 Bringing costing and cash flow together

The main points of this section are summarised in Figure 3.1 which shows the different ways in which costings are used in project planning and management. Clearly, planning the financial aspects of projects and events is an essential part of operational planning which we neglect at our peril. Unfortunately, although the basic ideas of costing and cash flow are straightforward, developing reliable forecasts of costs and cash flows for complicated projects (and *interpreting* them) presents some pitfalls for the inexperienced. The purpose here is to provide a subject overview rather than a detailed account of the technicalities of accounting, which are beyond the scope of this particular course. Most organisations will have a financial specialist on whose advice you can rely. To make the most of such advice, however, you need to understand enough about finance to ask the right questions.

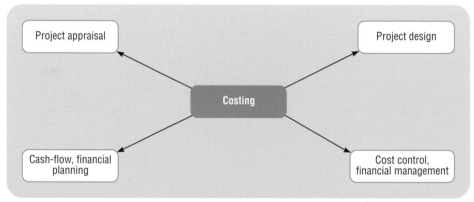

Figure 3.1 The uses of costing

ACTIVITY 3.1

Consider your organisation, or another that you know very well (for example, as a volunteer). How are costings and cash-flow statements for bids and proposals prepared? Are there procedures for having them 'signed off', for example?

_____

_____

_____

If, tomorrow, you had to prepare a costing and/or a cash-flow forecast for a project for which you were raising funds, or for an investment in a new form of fundraising (e.g. opening a new shop), how would you go about this and to whom would you turn for information and advice?

_____

_____

_____

Typically, costings and cash-flow forecasts are undertaken collaboratively – they involve bringing together information from several different areas. If you have been involved in such processes often before you will probably be quite familiar with what is involved. But if not, you might like to consider how you can start to gain experience in this area of work – perhaps by playing some part in the process, the next time a costing or cash-flow forecast is needed.

3.3 COSTING BIDS AND PROPOSALS

There are three broad areas to consider when deciding how to cost an application:

the first concerns estimating the direct and readily identifiable running costs in a reasonably discrete and self-contained proposal;

the second concerns the calculation and allocation of overheads and indirect costs in project applications;

the third concerns more general considerations about surpluses, losses and judgements of 'what the market will bear'.

These are dealt with in turn.

3.3.1 Costing discrete projects

A useful starting point is to consider how to identify costs in the case of a proposal which is largely self-contained and financially self-sufficient – as in the case of the hamburger stall.

A wide range of applications fall into this category. It includes many one-off applications for specific capital projects – a theatre company, for instance, which is seeking resources to improve its building or to upgrade its computerised box office. It also includes revenue projects, such as the case of a small community group applying for a single grant to employ a couple of workers in order to extend the scope of its operations. Similarly, an independent hostel tendering for a three-year contract to provide accommodation for homeless people, which will, in effect, constitute the whole of its work, falls into the category of a self-contained project for the purpose of estimating costs.

What these apparently very different applications have in common is the fact that, in each case, it is a reasonably straightforward matter to estimate the full costs of the proposed project or programme. The actual calculations may, of course, be complicated, but you will not need to take account of a range of contingent factors or additional external costs. Estimating the costs of such projects is primarily a matter of identifying the direct and the operating costs of a discrete, self-sufficient piece of work.

The costing process, in such circumstances, is essentially a much more elaborate version of what was involved in costing for the hamburger stall. Assuming that you aim to break even, it involves four steps:

1 identifying all the areas of expenditure
2 checking that you have not overlooked possible areas of expenditure
3 estimating the cost of each area of expenditure
4 adding it all up.

In making these calculations, you will need to take account of not just the direct costs of undertaking the proposed work (salaries, equipment, materials, and so on), but also, where appropriate, the identifiable and necessary support costs involved (rent, light and heat, management and administration). Box 3.1 lists some of the factors which can be overlooked in making a basic costing of a self-contained and self-sufficient proposal.

BOX 3.1

SOME HIDDEN AND EASILY FORGOTTEN COSTS

- communications (phone, letters)
- tax and national insurance
- administrative support
- travel and subsistence
- training
- maintenance and repairs
- purchase of publications
- conferences
- consultancy
- inflation
- salary increases/redundancy costs
- advertising and promotions
- irrecoverable VAT in the UK (or its equivalent in your country)
- depreciation
- hospitality
- equipment replacement
- 'winding-down' costs of time-limited projects

For any major application involving revenue costs – such as the hostel's application mentioned above – there are some complex calculations to be made about the balance between the proportion of the overall budget that should go on the provision of direct services and the proportion required for management and administrative support. Opinions vary about the balance; what is important is that you can justify the particular balance you make in your own case. (In this context, 20 per cent of an overall budget can be a perfectly reasonable amount for voluntary organisations to spend on administration and infrastructure.) You should certainly not be tempted to understate this area of cost just because you think it might make your application more acceptable to a potential funder.

up to 20% admin costs.

ACTIVITY 3.2

Assume you are the manager of the theatre company mentioned earlier. You plan to modernise your membership and mailing lists, your bookings records and your financial records through the purchase and installation of a suitable computer system.

1   When drawing up the case for this capital project and, in due course, a budget, which of the following areas of expenditure would you consider to be the most important?

    (a) hardware and software

    (b) furniture

    (c) maintenance contract

    (d) computer stationery

    (e) booking clerk's salary

    (f) consultancy

    (g) post and telephone costs

    (h) transfer of existing records to new system

2   Are there any other areas you think are important?

_____

_____

_____

There is clearly plenty of scope for the exercise of judgement in this sort of estimation of the costs of a single project or proposal. And if it is a large and complex proposal it will inevitably involve some complex judgements of how to balance up different areas of cost. Nevertheless, you can identify by this process all the different elements of what will be required to enable the project to go ahead.

3.3.2 Calculating and allocating overheads

What complicates the business of estimating costs is the fact that many of the applications you are likely to make will not be for wholly discrete or self-standing projects. They are for contributions towards existing work; they are for resources that will enable you to open up new projects and add new staff or facilities to your current range of operations; they may also be for replacements of resources you have lost so that you can continue providing the services wanted by your clients.

As far as the process of costing is concerned, there is a very important difference between, say, deciding on the resources you need to set up a brand new Islamic studies centre from scratch and estimating those you need to develop a faculty of Islamic studies in an existing university. How a small community group calculates the costs of setting up a new advice centre, employing two advice workers, will be different from how a branch of a national federal agency such as Citizens Advice works out the costs of adding two new advice workers to an existing staff team in an existing office. In the case of the new advice centre and the new Islamic studies centre, the process outlined above will, in principle, suffice to identify the costs of their plans and hence what they need to raise. In the case of adding the new faculty and the new Citizens Advice Bureau (CAB) staff, however, that procedure very quickly runs into some difficult problems.

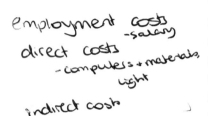

Take the case of the two new workers at the CAB. It is fairly easy to estimate their *employment costs* and such readily quantifiable additional *direct costs* as the equipment, materials, secretarial time, and so forth, that they will directly need to do their work. Beyond that, in the area of *indirect costs,* things are much less clear cut. Since there is no need for additional office accommodation, are there any additional rental costs? Since the photocopier rental and maintenance is already paid for, do they cost the CAB anything under this heading? They will certainly make some demands on personnel, finance and administration staff – but how should they be estimated for the purposes of identifying the costs of the two new workers? Similarly, they will require managing by the CAB manager and/or regional staff. But since the manager is already paid from elsewhere to develop and manage project staff, is it realistic to include a 'management charge' in the costings? How should one estimate the costs incurred by the two new staff members' use of national Citizens Advice wider training, promotions and publicity work?

These are all the sorts of cost considerations that fall into that catch-all category of 'overheads'. It is a source of some of the most difficult – and contentious – problems of costing. On the one hand, it is quite sensible for an organisation to ensure that any new project 'pays its way' and does not result in a net drain on your overall resources. Any new venture has cost implications for the existing organisation – especially for its core administrative and management operations. It is perfectly reasonable to want to build those additional costs into your project budget. On the other hand, it is fiendishly difficult to calculate and allocate such overhead costs with any degree of accuracy or agreement. If pursued too rigidly, it can result in project budgets which seem hopelessly unrealistic and unreasonable. Box 3.2 gives an example of what can happen when an organisation suddenly changes its procedures for calculating overheads and management costs.

BOX 3.2

THE OVERHEADS

I recently put together a funding application for £78,000 over 18 months, which included an estimation of the management and administration costs of the proposed project. I was then told that a new policy had been adopted and that, in future, all projects would have to pay a per capita contribution to the salaries of everyone in the administration section, the director, deputy director, fundraiser and promotions unit. This sum came to about the same cost as the salary of the project worker (£36,000 over 18 months). To my mind this made the project very unattractive to a potential funder and I did not proceed with it on that basis. Subsequently, a new director suggested that we calculate these overhead costs differently — at 20 per cent of project costs.

There is, sadly, no single convention or procedure for calculating and estimating the overhead costs of projects and programmes which build on the existing work and resources of an organisation. How you estimate the overheads for a particular application will depend on the wider policies, structures and financial systems of your organisation. There is, however, a simple continuum you can usefully bear in mind (See Figure 3.2).

Recovery of marginal costs   Recovery of full costs

Figure 3.2   The overheads (break-even) continuum

Let us start by assuming that you are basically aiming to break even. You want to secure sufficient resources to do what you propose to do without making a surplus on the deal or ending up with a shortfall which will have to be found from elsewhere in the existing organisation. In such circumstances, the overheads you need to include in your budget will fall somewhere along the continuum.

The marginal costs of any project are those additional, variable costs which are directly and identifiably incurred by the proposed project – salaries and related costs; additional materials; secretarial, administration and management time directly used by the project; and so forth. The full costs include the new project's contribution to the organisation's fixed costs (rent, lighting, insurance, publications, and so on) together with the costs incurred by all the other individuals and departments in the wider organisation which, in some way or other, have to service and help sustain its operations – and without whose work the project could not actually function as a wholly self-sufficient cost centre. Over and above the direct costs it incurs, it would also need to 'purchase' a wide range of indirect services and facilities from the rest of the organisation and these would all need to be estimated to give an indication of the full cost.

The UK's Association of Chief Executives of Voluntary Organisations (ACEVO) describes such 'core costs' (or overheads) as:

- 'the management costs of all activity
- the research and development capacity within voluntary organisations
- the support services – maintaining the premises, IT and finance costs – as well as the administrative, personnel and training costs.' (ACEVO, 2004, p. 8).

While insisting that all organisations in search of funding keep such costs to a minimum, ACEVO argues that funders and fundraisers need to be more transparent about the nature and vital importance of core costs, and to acknowledge that there is a level below which core costs cannot fall without endangering the sustainability of the funded organisation (and therefore the effectiveness of the funding itself).

As the example in Box 3.2 suggests, there may well be a significant difference in your budget depending on whether you are aiming in your application to secure no more than the marginal cost or whether, through the overheads, you are aiming to secure the (notionally) full cost of the project. Moreover, what will ensure you break even in one situation will not automatically ensure you break even in another. For instance, if such core services as management, administration support, training, and so on, are already funded by other grants or contracts, the recovery of marginal costs will be sufficient for you to break even. Alternatively, if those 'core costs' all have to be found and sustained from the overheads in a mixture of project contracts, then you are likely to need to make more of a 'full costs' calculation to ensure that you break even.

Similarly, overheads which ensure you break even will vary if you are seeking resources for a project requiring the appointment of additional staff or if you aim to provide a new or additional area of work for an existing team whose current project is coming to an end. The 'management charge' needed to buy out one-fifth of a manager's time will not be the same as one which simply enables her to supervise another project coordinator who is in charge of his own budget.

ACTIVITY 3.3

Think about a project that, given the opportunity, you might wish to develop for an organisation of your choice.

(a) What are likely to be the main areas of expenditure?

_____

_____

_____

(b) What are the overheads it will incur?

_____

_____

_____

(c) How will you allocate these?

_____

_____

_____

(d) What adjustments might you have to make to these?

_____

_____

_____

Obviously this will vary from project to project, but revisit Box 3.1 to check that you have not missed any hidden costs. It is generally not good employment practice to assume that costs can be kept down by offering lower salaries. In an economic climate of full employment, voluntary organisations can face recruitment problems. Equally, skimping on operating costs can limit the ability of workers to do the job, and cutting out what are often seen as 'extras' such as training and buying publications will limit the development of staff and their ability to scan the environment.

3.3.3 From costing to pricing

The discussions of estimating costs and calculating overheads above both assumed that your main concern in costing a project for an application is to break even. There are, of course, other considerations which may influence your costings and lead you to make adjustments to the budget you submit with your application. For instance, if you were very keen to open up a new area of work and were in a position to invest resources from elsewhere in your own organisation in a particular venture, you might choose to prepare a budget which covered less than the marginal costs. The project would technically run at a loss, but it would be a way of developing your experience and standing in that field with a view to securing more adequate funding in the future. By the same token, you might be invited to undertake a piece of work which you did not really have the time or interest in pursuing at that particular time. In such circumstances, it might be worth your while continuing only if you could actually generate some additional income from the deal; you might decide, therefore, to put in an application with a budget at more than full cost.

Even if you are not concerned to generate a surplus on a particular project, it is nevertheless useful to consider the resources you need to ensure that it can be sustained satisfactorily. If you want to move beyond an endless succession of discrete one-off projects, part of any management charge will need to be devoted to extending projects and the transitions between them. (And, incidentally, don't forget that even a time-limited venture always requires some winding-down costs.)

Given that there is always going to be some elasticity in the calculation and the subsequent management of overheads, you can often adjust your budget in the light of your assessment of a potential partner's ability to provide you with the resources you need. At the end of the day, all estimates of costs depend on wider judgements about the state of the 'market' and not just on technical calculations. Take the case of the fee you fix for a sponsorship agreement. Getting the level right involves not only costing out the services provided, but judging how much companies would be prepared to pay for certain benefits. Such broadly defined judgements of 'what the market will bear' apply in the case of costings for an application just as they do in other types of financial calculation.

So, costing is an art not a science. As with all other aspects of asking for resources and support, choosing how much to ask for will depend on who you are applying to and your own assessment of what is appropriate and feasible for your own organisation. In deciding on the most appropriate budget for a particular project, the skills you exercise are not just those of mathematics, but primarily those of assessment, presentation and negotiation, which are the mainstay of the rest of your work in fundraising and campaigning more generally.

ACTIVITY 3.4

Thinking of your own organisation, or another you know well (perhaps as a volunteer), how are overheads allocated and prices determined for bids and proposals? Are there explicit policies and procedures for handling the more controversial aspects? How much flexibility is there?

If, tomorrow, you were asked to prepare a costing and a price for a project for which you were bidding or raising funds, how would you go about this, and to whom would you turn for information and advice?

As with Activity 3.1, these questions involve bringing together information from several different areas, and perhaps judgements about future trends and strategic possibilities for an organisation. If you have been involved in such discussions before you will probably be familiar with how these issues are tackled. But if not, you might like to consider how you can start to gain experience in these important areas of work – perhaps by sitting in on a meeting or by having a role in the team that prepares a tender. This might be something to discuss with your line manager when your future training and development are next being considered.

3.4 EVALUATING FINANCIAL PERFORMANCE IN FUNDRAISING

This section is about deciding how successful your fundraising activities have been. It's about evaluating the financial performance of particular events, programmes, campaigns or regions – or indeed of the fundraising department as a whole. For anyone new to fundraising this may sound easy – surely you just count up the money received, subtract what you spent on raising it and compare it to your target? As you will see, it is not that simple. Indeed, this topic quickly leads into a nest of complex and sometimes controversial issues. For this reason, all we can do is provide an introduction to the topic and an overview of the main considerations that you as a fundraiser will need to bear in mind.

3.4.1 Monitoring or review?

Evaluation can take place in different ways and at different points in the fundraising cycle, even though it is usually conceived of as the final stage. To avoid confusion, we will use the term *assessment* for evaluations that look forward – that is, appraising and choosing between options for how to go about raising money. One use of the costings discussed earlier is in assessing different fundraising options. For the kind of evaluation which goes on during a particular activity to make sure it is on course, we will use the term *monitoring.* For the kind of 'stock taking' evaluation which happens at the end of an activity, *review* is the most appropriate term: literally a 'looking back' (a re-view) – that asks not just 'are we doing things right?' but 'are we doing the right things?'

Two considerations drive evaluation activities. The first is the need for *external* reporting and accountability – being able to demonstrate sound stewardship of public, charitable or members' funds. The second consideration driving evaluation is for *internal* learning and improvement – so that fundraisers can understand what worked (or didn't work), and why. The distinctions between monitoring and review and between internal and external reporting give us four different contexts in which the results of fundraising may be reported and discussed. This is shown in Table 3.4.

Table 3.4 Contexts for reporting the results of fundraising	Monitoring	Review
Internal – control, improvement and learning		
External – accountability		

ACTIVITY 3.5

How does your organisation (or another that you know well) carry out the four different types of financial reporting and evaluation in Table 3.4? What information does it use for internal purposes, and what does it provide for external use?

Make notes here and in Table 3.4.

Monthly reports

Monthly accounts

Quarterly finance meetings - reforcasting

Annual plans

Team meetings to check progress against plans

BUT - v. little concrete analysis is com. fund.
Limelight reviewed, broken down
Lots of immeasurable factors - gen. awareness leading to com fund

Comparing monthly results with the budget and cash-flow forecast (as discussed earlier in this session) is the most common method of *internal monitoring*. Likewise, any forecasts presented as part of an application for funding will provide a basis against which your progress may be checked by that funder (*external monitoring*). Many organisations provide regular reports on progress to supporters in other ways – a classic example is the large visual display of progress towards a target (in the form of a thermometer, or a gauge of some kind).

Internal reviews of fundraising are undertaken in different ways, but if they are done thoroughly they usually involve some comparisons and information about external trends. The information provided for *external review* is presented in annual financial accounts and reporting.

Monitoring by managing budgets can sometimes involve difficult judgements – in particular, whether and in what way to intervene if things are not going according to plan and some form of corrective action seems to be needed. However, it is the issues associated with review that are the most challenging and controversial for fundraisers. And these issues also provide an important part of the context and focus for monitoring. Hence, this section is mainly focused on review.

3.4.2 Reviewing financial performance: the need for indicators

A major difficulty in reviewing financial performance arises from the delays between fundraising activities and money received. This is most obvious with legacy fundraising. You could run a legacy campaign that attracts great interest and leads to a significant number of new and existing supporters notifying your charity that they have made a provision for your cause in their will, and yet it is quite possible that, a year later, you may still not have received a single bequest. Likewise, many organisations will, from time to time, run campaigns to attract new donors and supporters. These campaigns can be expensive, and it would not be at all unusual for the cost of acquiring the new donors to be about the same as the amount contributed by those new donors in response to the campaign. So are such campaigns expensive failures – if they make little or no net contribution to the cause? The answer is almost certainly not – because the organisation has acquired, not just some one-off donations, but the makings of a new cohort of committed supporters. If properly nurtured, many of these donors will continue to give, regularly or intermittently, for years to come.

In other words, many fundraising activities are actually a sort of investment: when successful, the organisation is building up an asset – its legacy file, its donor list – that should generate a flow of income in future years. This is fine, not least because it makes future flows of voluntary income a bit more predictable (and thus makes it easier to plan the organisation's activities in an efficient and effective manner). But it significantly complicates the job of reviewing financial performance. To a considerable extent, the success of a fundraising department in the current year reflects past efforts and achievements. The current manager and staff are harvesting the goodwill, loyalty and relationships built up by their predecessors over many years. But equally, if you say that although you do not have much net income to show for your efforts this year, you have acquired lots of new supporters, so the future is bright – is that good news or bad news? And how can anyone tell?

What is needed in such situations is a way of estimating the likely contribution these new donors will make in the future. For example, if most of the new donors that you have recruited over

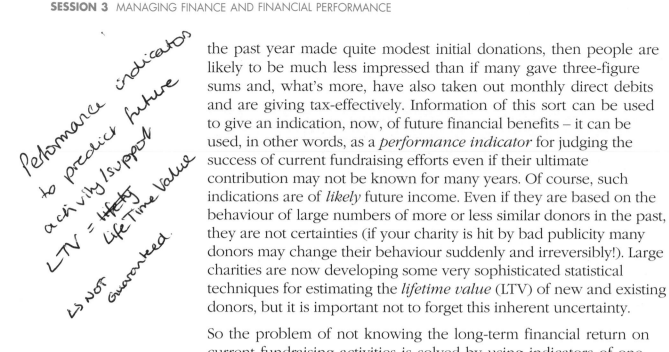

the past year made quite modest initial donations, then people are likely to be much less impressed than if many gave three-figure sums and, what's more, have also taken out monthly direct debits and are giving tax-effectively. Information of this sort can be used to give an indication, now, of future financial benefits – it can be used, in other words, as a *performance indicator* for judging the success of current fundraising efforts even if their ultimate contribution may not be known for many years. Of course, such indications are of *likely* future income. Even if they are based on the behaviour of large numbers of more or less similar donors in the past, they are not certainties (if your charity is hit by bad publicity many donors may change their behaviour suddenly and irreversibly!). Large charities are now developing some very sophisticated statistical techniques for estimating the *lifetime value* (LTV) of new and existing donors, but it is important not to forget this inherent uncertainty.

So the problem of not knowing the long-term financial return on current fundraising activities is solved by using indicators of one kind or another. These may involve doing clever things with powerful computers and large databases, but often they are simple and straightforward: for example, the *cost per donor acquired* can be used to appraise different ways of attracting new supporters. And if you want to know whether your donor list is in better shape at the end of the year than at the start, then comparing it with last year, in terms not just of the number of supporters but of the *frequency* (number of donations), the *recency* (how long since the most recent donation) and the *value* of the donations they are making, will give you a pretty good idea of what is happening.

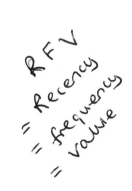

'RFV', as these indicators are collectively termed, is a very useful concept. More comprehensive yet, Lifetime Value calculations draw on a charity's experience with similar donors in the past to calculate what the likely net contribution from a donor will be over, say, five years. Net contribution here means donations after the cost of fundraising and donor communications has been deducted. LTV fits with the idea of long-term engagement with donors, what Burnett (2002) calls 'relationship fundraising'. To work out LTV the charity forecasts the likely cost of the fundraising and communication programme which it will direct at the donor each year, and subtracts this sum from its estimate of the donor's total gifts for each year. Adding up the resulting set of annual net contributions gives a figure which can be used as the basis for calculating the value of the donor over time in today's money.

You might ask: why not just use the figure as it is? But remember that cash in the present is worth a great deal more than estimated income in the future. Not only is this because of risk and uncertainty, but also inflation and the opportunity cost of what else you could do over a period of time with the money you spend on fundraising from individuals. You could instead, for example, have invested the money in an interest-earning deposit account over five years. In order to reflect the way that money in the future has less value than money in the present, a discount factor is applied to each year's projected contribution to bring it into line with the present value of money. The further into the future, the greater the need to adjust. Table 3.5 provides a simple example which helps explain this basically simple approach to valuing donors.

Table 3.5   Lifetime value calculation to show 'present value' of an individual donor over five years.

	Year 1	Year 2	Year 3	Year 4	Year 5	Total
Income						
Cash	80	90				170
Raffles	10	12	15	20	10	67
Direct debit with GiftAid			80	80	120	280
Total income from donor	**90**	**102**	**95**	**100**	**130**	**517**
Costs						
Direct mail appeals	5	10	5	8	8	36
Newsletter	4	4	5	6	6	25
Raffles	2	2	3	4	4	15
Total costs	**11**	**16**	**13**	**18**	**18**	**76**
Contribution	*79*	*86*	*82*	*82*	*112*	*441*
Discounted value	*79*	*78.2*	*67.8*	*61.6*	*76.5*	*363.1*
(using rate of 10% per annum)						

This donor appears to like raffles, and may have been persuaded by a direct mail appeal in Year 2 to start giving by direct debit tax-effectively and then to increase the regular amount in Year 5. The decision to use a 10% discount rate (based on this particular charity's assumptions about inflation, risk and opportunity costs) means that the unadjusted contribution in year 2 is 110% of its 'real' present value, in year 3 is 121% of that value, in year 4 is 133% and so on. To save the trouble of working out the factors to apply, there are published tables of discounting factors at different levels.

Sargeant and Jay (2004, p. 149) point to the usefulness of LTV analysis not only for valuing individual donors but for estimating the value of entire segments. Knowing the value of donors who have been recruited via different channels can lead to better decisions about what media to use to recruit donors in future. It also becomes easier to justify how much to spend on finding new donors. If you think in terms of a five-year relationship, you might be prepared to spend more on recruitment in the hope of attracting high-spending donors who will repay the investment handsomely in the longer term. LTV calculations also help in deciding what kind of marketing programme to offer a particular segment, and in where best to target effort in order to reactivate lapsed donors.

ACTIVITY 3.6

Thinking about your own organisation, or another with which you are very familiar, what indicators are used to judge the success of fundraising activities in situations when the *immediate* cash return is not the only, or the principal, consideration? What difficulties do these indicators introduce?

_____

_____

_____

Some indicators may be quantitative, others may be qualitative and more a matter of impressions. Whatever the indicators you use, they probably give rise to some debates – over how reliable they are, how to interpret them and how much weight to give to different indicators if some are looking much more positive than others.

3.4.3 Comparisons and the idea of benchmarking

Creating measures and indicators of performance is one thing. Interpreting what they mean is another. For example, how do you decide if a cost of £12.34 per enquiry is good, bad or indifferent? In the end, the answer always comes down to comparisons. If £12.34 per enquiry was the result achieved by your advertisement in one magazine, whereas the same advertisement in other publications achieved results in the range £5–£10 per enquiry, then obviously it doesn't look too good. Alternatively, if £12.34 is the average cost for the campaign this year, and last year the average cost was £14.08, then that is an improvement. And those *internal* comparisons – between different contexts (groups, media, lists, regions, etc.) where the same thing has been tried, and between this year and earlier years – are pretty well universal in examining and interpreting fundraising results, as they are in evaluating results in other areas of organisational activity.

However, in recent years the limitations of only making internal comparisons have been widely recognised. Perhaps you are doing a bit better than before – but actually, you are still way below what is being achieved by others. Or perhaps your performance has declined slightly this year – but this reflects a wider trend and others have fared much worse. You will not know unless you compare your results with those of other more or less comparable organisations

It is useful to distinguish two ways in which such comparisons can be made.

First, there are public comparisons published in trade magazines, yearbooks or sometimes on websites (for example, in the UK, the annual 'league table' of charity shop performance published by the magazine *Charity Finance*). These may be based on survey responses or on the figures contained in annual reports and in returns to regulatory bodies like the Charity Commission. Such comparisons are often rough-and-ready exercises, comparing results across a few measures of overall performance. They are often more interesting for the overall trends they reveal compared with previous years than the particular rankings that come out of them.

The second way such comparisons are undertaken is in confidential benchmarking exercises. The idea here is that a group of organisations get together to compare in detail how they carry out a particular process, in order to identify the more successful methods that may be adopted by others to improve performance. Such benchmarking usually involves some measurement – in order to identify which organisations seem to carry out particular parts of the process well. However, such comparisons can be difficult and time-consuming. It's not just that the organisations will each have their own mix and scale of fundraising activities; each organisation also has its own idiosyncratic way of keeping track of costs. So setting out the costs and income associated with different sorts of fundraising, in a way that allows meaningful comparisons between all those involved, is no easy exercise. As anyone who has been involved in such exercises knows, the bigger the apparent differences in performance the more likely it is that they are explained in part by different ways of allocating costs!

Benchmarking = comparisons with other external organisations.

Be wary of diff ways of allocating costs

However, the aim is not just to make comparisons or to show who is best. The aim is performance improvement, achieved through adopting and adapting the methods used by those who are successful. And this can still be achieved even if the measurements are estimates that need to be interpreted cautiously. Because such exercises are confidential – and people are able to speak freely – benchmarking clubs are the best way to obtain detailed, high-quality information on how things are done, and the actual results achieved, in relatively successful organisations comparable to your own.

In UK fundraising, the annual 'Fundratios' exercise, run by the Institute of Fundraising and the Centre for Interfirm Comparison, is the main benchmarking club for fundraisers (Institute of Fundraising, 2007). Table 3.6 reproduces one of the tables provided to participants in a recent year and gives an idea of the level of detail that is involved. Note, however, that such information comes at a price – not just the fee charged to join the club but the cost of staff time in preparing a detailed return from which the comparisons can be calculated. Whether this is worthwhile for a particular charity will depend on many factors. In particular, what matters is whether, and in what ways, members of a benchmarking club *use* the information – to identify areas of possible weakness and to identify others from whom they are likely to learn improved procedures, systems and approaches.

Table 3.6 Fundraising cost effectiveness

Ratio No.		2	3	5	6	7	9	10	15	17	18
INCOME RAISED PER £1 INVESTED FOR EACH ACTIVITY											
21 Central Fundraising											
a) Corporate	£	2.78	11.98	2.33	1.54	5.18	3.27	4.71	3.30	4.08	3.02
b) Trusts	£	4.23	21.53	12.12	5.16	4.97	7.25	9.57	7.09	11.06	7.72
c) Legacies	£	70.43	30.20	40.72	26.02	36.18	52.28	66.58	10.29	48.59	124.44
d) Competitions (including Lotteries)	£	1.56	1.91	–	1.64	51.67	3.22	–	5.44	2.31	3.80
e) Special Events	£	5.35	1.86	5.76	1.58	4.87	1.68	1.29	1.88	2.05	1.26
f) Membership	£	–	–	–	–	–	–	–	–	–	4.15
g) Direct Marketing Appeals	£	1.64	6.25	2.41	3.22	2.75	1.46	3.91	1.79	2.02	–
h) Committed Giving	£	4.00	3.79	2.29	4.85	4.05	2.06	2.60	3.49	36.47	1.35
i) House to House (if organised centrally)	£	–	1.57	–	4.02	–	4.09	–	4.35	–	–
j) TOTAL Central Fundraising	£	**6.41**	**2.73**	**5.72**	**3.92**	**5.49**	**4.78**	**3.26**	**4.46**	**5.81**	**22.50**
22 Local Fundraising											
a) House to House (not organised centrally)	£	5.98	–	22.80	–	12.47	–	45.85	–	2.00	8.48
b) Schools/Youth	£	1.30	–	–	–	na	1.34	na	–	–	–
c) All other local income	£	1.86	8.89	1.55	na	1.41	0.64	3.09	12.44	1.32	2.47
d) TOTAL Local Fundraising	£	**1.86**	**8.89**	**1.69**	**na**	**–**	**0.84**	**3.32**	**12.44**	**1.43**	**2.63**
23 a) Other	£	–	–	5.76	–	–	–	–	25.75	–	0.11
Voluntary Income Raised	£	**5.37**	**5.09**	**4.29**	**4.31**	**4.39**	**3.87**	**5.59**	**5.35**	**3.52**	**11.44**

3.4.4 Accountability and fundraising costs

A journalist working for a Scottish Sunday paper phoned the Open University following a major scandal concerning a breast-cancer charity. He wanted to write a piece sympathetic to charities to help restore public confidence in their fundraising activities. In preparing for this he had visited the Caritas Data website which uses publicly available charity accounts to show comparative costs in fundraising – and he had been horrified by the figures he saw there. He phoned the University as part of his efforts to work out what was really going on. You can read the results of his inquiries in Box 3.3.

BOX 3.3

SCOTTISH CHARITIES IN FURY OVER DATABASE

Some of Scotland's biggest charities fear 'misleading' accountancy figures published on a UK-wide database could have cost them thousands in lost donations.

Information on the National Charities Database, which includes the accounts of every major charity in Britain, implied that with some, less than 15p in every pound raised was going towards good causes.

High-profile organisations implicated included Capability Scotland, Cornerstone Community Care and Aberlour Child Care Trust. The horrified charities were unaware these figures had been made publicly available until this was pointed out by the *Sunday Post*. They immediately vowed to contact the database company to request a correction.

Despite initially refusing to change the data, and insisting to us that it was accurate, the publisher appeared to back down last week and by Friday the information had been altered.

The database is visited by 1.2 million people every month and is used by companies, trusts and individuals who may be planning to make a charitable donation. It is administered by a firm called Caritas Data, a highly respected London-based business information publisher, and is the largest charities database of its type in the UK.

It appeared to show some charities had alarmingly high costs for fundraising. For example, it stated the ratio for Capability Scotland is 85.5 per cent, suggesting that for every £1 the charity receives from the public, 85.5p is eaten up by costs, with just 14.5p going to good causes.

Capability Scotland's Director of Finance, Richard Hellewell, was appalled. 'This ratio is not accurate and should be 23 per cent. The fact it was being publicised had the potential to do serious damage to our reputation,' he fumed. ➡

Ian Yule, of special needs charity Cornerstone Community Care, said, 'The figures on this database were very misleading and caused us a great deal of concern. We fear they may have done serious damage to our reputation.'

Nigel Fairhead, of Aberlour Child Care Trust, added, 'This tool is used by the public and the voluntary sector. We're unhappy with the misleading way the statistics were presented.'

Lucy McTernan, of the Scottish Council for Voluntary Organisations, claimed the ratios published were flawed, misleading and inappropriate. 'This database is potentially very damaging to the voluntary sector,' she added. 'The Breast Cancer Research scandal has raised a lot of doubts about charities in Scotland and this type of misleading information does not help. It proves the need for a readily available database of Scottish charities. This subject has to be included as part of the charity law reform agenda.

Professor Rob Paton, a charity accounts expert at the Open University, said, 'This situation is dangerous and I have sympathy for the charities implicated. Databases such as this have been taken to court in America and I would not like to see that happen here.'

But the initial response by Alan Rattigan, Managing Director of Caritas Data, was that he didn't believe the database figures were wrong. 'It depends on whose opinion you take,' he explained. 'We won't change the ratios if they are not incorrect. However, if we find a mistake has been made we will hold our hands up.'

Since making that statement, the information on the company's website has been changed. Mr Rattigan did not respond when we attempted to speak to him again.

Last night, Capability Scotland's Director of Communications, Michelle Hegarty, thanked the *Sunday Post* for bringing the matter to their attention. She added, 'We are very relieved the database is now publishing accurate figures.'

A spokesman for the Scottish Executive said the setting up of a publicly available database will be a matter for the new Charities Regulator, who will be announced later this year. He added, 'This is something that will be looked at and we will consider passing legislation to bring it in.'

(Source: Harrison, 2003)

The interesting thing about this case is that both sides may have been right! The figures could have been technically correct – and still highly misleading. Such situations – and they are becoming increasingly common – arise for a number of reasons. For example, if the costs and income of charity shops are included within 'fundraising', this would sharply increase the costs per pound raised. The reasons are obvious. If you buy a new or second-hand article in a charity shop you know perfectly well that the surplus for the charity will be much lower than if you had made a pure donation of the same sum. And it doesn't bother you – you are getting a benefit and understand that the shop incurs considerable costs. What's more, retailing involves commercial risks – the fortunes of charity shops tend to rise and fall depending on many factors including the local competition, the strength of the local groups supporting the shops, the retailing expertise of those managing the operations, and so on. For such reasons, charities that have relied heavily on shops as a source of income will, quite properly, have much higher fundraising costs than other charities.

Other factors that can affect the reported fundraising ratio are major investments in fundraising (e.g. investing in new computer systems or a drive to recruit new supporters); and how a charity accounts for related activities like campaigning and education. This latter question is particularly difficult and important. For example, charities often undertake activities to promote their cause which have a fundraising dimension, but which might not be justified purely in fundraising terms. How do they allocate the costs involved? One charity may shrewdly, even opportunistically, allocate a large part of the costs to education and campaigning, so reducing the apparent cost of fundraising in its annual report. Another, for simplicity but perhaps naively, may leave most or all the costs of such activities to be counted as fundraising – so increasing the overall cost of fundraising. For internal management purposes this second approach is unlikely to matter – everyone understands what is going on, and the need to justify the event in non-financial terms will be obvious. But when these same figures are published externally for accountability purposes, they may be used in public comparisons with the first organisation – and the results will look awful. This lack of attention to the way figures look will affect the way a funder views your application for support.

So, as with the issue of costing and the allocation of overheads when you are seeking external funding, 'the cost of fundraising' turns out to be a difficult and potentially contentious issue. A range of answers is likely to be possible and defensible, depending on how the figures are going to be used. And fundraisers need to think how their reported fundraising costs will look to others outside the organisation. Public websites now offer ratings and league tables based on published accounts. Such systems can be used by donors and funders to assess the financial health of organisations they may assist. But you do not know which of your figures will be used and which other organisations you will be compared with. In the face of these worrying uncertainties it is easy to feel aggrieved: your job is difficult enough without facing ill-informed criticism from self-appointed champions of accountability. But such a response is dangerous in the extreme. You cannot expect the public (or journalists) to be experts on the costing issues that surround fundraising; nevertheless, they are fully entitled to know how much you spend on it. And it is your job to maintain the bond of trust both with the public at large and your supporters in particular.

So charities need to do two things. First, they need to check carefully how much they are really spending on fundraising (has proper allowance been made for all the main overheads?) and where necessary they must clean up their practice ('would I want to give to a charity that spent that much on fundraising?' is a good start). Second, they need to get their stories straight. This means reporting their costs and income in ways that are meaningful and comprehensible to supporters, and being ready to explain, compare and justify their costs. These are not simple issues and in most organisations they are likely to involve people from other parts of the organisation – including, possibly, the trustees. But as a fundraiser it is important that you play a full part in the discussions over your organisation's policies on these matters.

ACTIVITY 3.7

Make notes on the questions below.

(a) Thinking of your organisation or one with which you are familiar (perhaps as a volunteer), how alert is it to the issues discussed above?

_____

_____

_____

_____

_____

(b) Are you satisfied in your own mind that the amount spent by the organisation on fundraising is appropriate? What evidence is there that your supporters would find it acceptable? Does the organisation have a policy that its ratio will not exceed a certain amount (and if so, how is the ratio calculated – does it include overheads, for example)? If not, should it have such a policy?

_____

_____

_____

_____

_____

(c) How are the costs of fundraising reported by the organisation? How do they compare with other organisations in its field? What steps has the organisation taken to ensure that its figures appear reasonable and can be understood? What else could it do?

_____

_____

_____

_____

_____

_____

These are all very broad questions and we don't expect that you will be able to answer them comprehensively! They do, however, raise relevant and important issues for reflection. Book 1's coverage of accountability is worth reviewing in the context of this session – particularly the collaborative opportunities it offers charities to present a united front in explaining how fundraising works and how it needs to be adequately resourced in order to continue to provide benefits both to donors and the organisations they support.

3.5 SUMMARY

Here is a summary of the main learning points from this session:

- Costing is essentially a common-sense procedure involving the identification of all the relevant items of expenditure in a project, estimating or establishing the relevant amounts, and coming to a total. It becomes more complicated for complex and uncertain elements.

- Costing allows you to:
  - assess if an event or project is worthwhile
  - design activities to optimise success
  - create a budget and targets for monitoring purposes.

- Cash-flow management coordinates the timing of expenses flowing out of an organisation and income flowing in.

- The three broad areas to consider when deciding how to cost an application for funding are:
  - estimating or establishing the direct, identifiable running costs of the proposal
  - calculating and allocating overheads or indirect costs
  - judging what the market will bear and the required level of return for the organisation on the activity concerned.

- Financial evaluation of fundraising fulfils the need for external accountability and internal learning. Such evaluation includes monitoring (ongoing comparison of performance against targets) and review (one-off stock taking).

- Financial evaluation of fundraising is complicated by the lapse of time between fundraising activity and results (e.g. for legacy campaigns). Relevant performance indicators for fundraising include lifetime value of new and existing donors, cost per donor acquired, and frequency, recency and value of donations made.

- Performance comparisons can be made with publicly available information on similar organisations, or through private 'benchmarking' arrangements whereby groups of organisations share information to identify and emulate best practice.

- The ratio of cost to income in fundraising ('the fundraising ratio') varies widely between different situations and reporting conventions. Charities need to monitor such costs actively, and report cost and income in ways which are meaningful and comprehensible.

ACTIVITY 3.8

How important is an understanding of financial management and analysis in your work? And how competent do you consider yourself in the areas covered in this session?

(a) Estimating direct costs _____

_____

(b) Estimating indirect costs _____

_____

(c) Creating and using cash-flow forecasts _____

_____

(d) Making decisions about the allocation of overhead costs in external bids _____

_____

(e) Budgetary management _____

_____

(f) Choosing measures of financial performance for particular fundraising activities _____

_____

(g) Checking the relationship between the financial flows associated with fundraising activities and the way they are shown in financial reports (e.g. by asking how, when and where costs and income have been recorded in management accounts) _____

_____

(h) Comparing your fundraising costs and returns with those of other organisations _____

_____

(i) Anticipating, and navigating an honourable way through, issues surrounding the cost of fundraising in your organisation. As the fundraiser you are accountable not only to your organisation but also to the funder who has trusted you with their support.

(j) If you are aware of a shortfall, how do you cope? What steps might you take to develop your competence?

You may not have to do much financial planning and management, if you have other people to whom you can turn. However, you will still have to recognise when to ask for help, and contribute your understanding of the proposed activities to the costing of a project. So you will have to be involved, and this is one obvious way of developing your competence and understanding in this area. A common mistake where figures are involved is that people who think they are 'no good with finances' try to have as little to do with finance as possible – and this simply reinforces their weakness in financial matters.

Evaluation: Completing the Fundraising Cycle

CONTENTS

4 EVALUATION: COMPLETING THE FUNDRAISING CYCLE

4.1 INTRODUCTION

It is satisfying to see an event run smoothly, or to launch an initiative on time and within budget. But was it all worthwhile? And how do you know? Did the event do what it was supposed to? Did the right people attend? Would it be worth repeating next year? Was the initiative a good use of resources? What lessons can we learn?

Making it happen is one thing. It is often very hard to tell whether a particular fundraising approach, a method of working or an administrative practice is as effective as it might be. Showing that it was worthwhile or seeing how it can be done even better next time, is another – and the focus of this session.

Aims and learning outcomes

The three main aims of the session are:

- to develop understanding of different approaches to evaluation
- to identify the focus of different types of evaluation
- to explore the implications of using different measures of performance.

After studying this session you should be able to:

- explain the value of evaluation
- understand different approaches to evaluation – assessment, monitoring and review
- identify the focus of different types of evaluation and suggest the appropriate type of evaluation for a range of different situations
- debate the issues involved in using a range of measures of performance and quantitative approaches to evaluation.

ACTIVITY 4.1

Read the three scenarios below and, against each one, make a note of the kind of questions you would want to ask to find out what actually happened, so that you could make some sort of judgement about the degree of success in each case.

Scenario 1

The UK-based Medical Foundation for the Care of Victims of Torture planned a novel fundraising auction. 'The Immortality Auction' invited members of the public to place bids online, using a commercial sponsor's website, and at a final auction event held at the British Academy for Film and Television Arts. People were bidding for the chance to see their names appear in print – as a character in a book written by a best-selling author.

how many bids placed online? value?
publicity? attendance at event?
rel. with sponsors good/bad
time invested + RoI

Scenario 2

The Robben Island Museum, a world heritage site in South Africa, was asked by Nelson Mandela to host the 'Mandela SOS' concert to raise funds for the global crisis of HIV/AIDS. The concert was to feature live performances from some of the world's best-known recording artists, with Nelson Mandela himself attending and footage from the concert being broadcast simultaneously to a further event at the Green Point Stadium.

Scenario 3

The Big Issue in the North produces the *Big Issue* newspaper, which is sold by homeless vendors in return for keeping a percentage of the cover price. The organisation planned a Christmas appeal where they sent out cards thanking people for their support and asking them to send the card back with a message to *Big Issue* vendors and a donation.

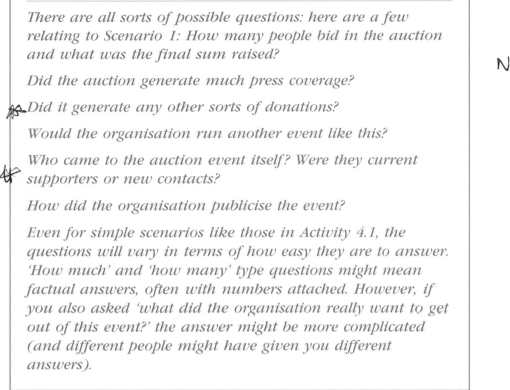

There are all sorts of possible questions: here are a few relating to Scenario 1: How many people bid in the auction and what was the final sum raised?

Did the auction generate much press coverage?

Did it generate any other sorts of donations?

Would the organisation run another event like this?

Who came to the auction event itself? Were they current supporters or new contacts?

How did the organisation publicise the event?

Even for simple scenarios like those in Activity 4.1, the questions will vary in terms of how easy they are to answer. 'How much' and 'how many' type questions might mean factual answers, often with numbers attached. However, if you also asked 'what did the organisation really want to get out of this event?' the answer might be more complicated (and different people might have given you different answers).

New support generated?

In the next section we look at exactly why it is important to ask questions like these to evaluate resource-winning activities.

4.2 WHY ASK QUESTIONS? THE IMPORTANCE OF EVALUATION

There is, of course, more to asking questions like those in Activity 4.1 above than just wanting to know what happened. Thinking about why we want to know more should help in working out what the most useful questions are.

This is similar to asking 'Why have company accounts?'. In general terms, there are two kinds of reasons, and they both also apply to evaluation as considered in this session. Evaluation is important, first, in order to discharge accountability, and, second, to help in making choices and improvements.

4.2.1 Accountability

Accountability relates to the idea of 'stewardship', whereby those who raise funds are held responsible for using those funds for the purposes stated in the appeal. The very word 'accounts' points to the importance of accountability. Similarly, those who run a fundraising event or campaign are accountable, first to their immediate managers, then to a set of stakeholders, including trustees, donors, volunteers, clients, and so on, and finally to society at large. These stakeholders also need to know that there has been no improper use of resources and that there is a result of value to them. (This can also be thought of in terms of seeing a 'return' on an 'investment' – though not a financial return. It could, for example, be a 'return' in terms of satisfaction at seeing progress towards a humanitarian goal on an 'investment' of time and effort as a volunteer.)

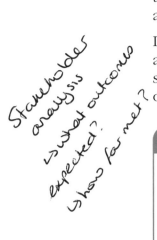

In general, when considering what kinds of questions to ask in an evaluation, it is useful to apply a 'stakeholder analysis' to the situation. This means thinking about who has a stake in the outcome and what they might need to know.

ACTIVITY 4.2

Using the three scenarios from Activity 4.1, note down the main stakeholders in each case.

Scenario 1

_____

_____

_____

_____

Scenario 2

_____

_____

_____

_____

Scenario 3

_____

_____

_____

Now look back at your list of questions from Activity 4.1 and note to what extent answering these questions would be useful in discharging your accountability to each of the stakeholders.

_____

_____

_____

_____

➡

Again, there are many possible answers. Here are some thoughts relating to Scenario 2: the 'SOS Concert' can be thought of as having many stakeholders, including the museum staff, management and board members, the recording artists who donated their services, those who attended, the organisations in the HIV/AIDS field who might benefit from the funds raised and, of course, the communities, families and individuals with whom they work.

Apart from having an interest in how much money was raised, different groups might like answers to slightly different questions. Museum board members might want to know how much the concert increased awareness of the museum and its role. Those attending might want to ask: 'Does a large proportion of the money raised actually get to people with HIV/AIDS? Is the amount spent on organising this event kept relatively low?'

4.2.2 Making choices and improvements

When we start asking questions about fundraising events or campaigns, it is a short step from 'Did we do better than last year?' to questions with practical implications:

- Which parts went particularly well? What could have been done better?
- Should we do the same again? Charge more? Target the publicity differently?

As well as asking questions that may help with deciding what to do now, it is also useful to build up information that may not be used straight away but will be available in the future. Collecting significant data in all areas this year means that you will not have to rely on memory should you need to check on something next year.

At the same time, too much data can be just as bad as too little if there is no easy way to analyse it. It often helps to start with the decisions you know you have some control over and then work back from these to determine which of many possible questions to ask in your evaluation.

For instance, in Scenario 3 there are all kinds of questions you might ask about the people who responded to the Big Issue in the North Appeal: How many came from which parts of the region? Were they regular supporters? Were there any significant donations made? How many donations were from individuals and how many were corporate? If there is the possibility of targeting particular groups in order to increase donations from individuals of that type, then questions aimed at knowing which groups are the best prospect would be particularly useful. Alternatively, if there is a proposal to have two appeals next year, one for each of two parts of the region, then questions about where the respondents come from might give useful information to aid that decision.

Apart from relating to real future options, the kinds of questions that help in making choices can be those where the answers lead to understanding about which aspects of an event or campaign worked best (or didn't work), and what it was about them that made them work. In other words, in addition to the quantitative 'How much?' or 'How many of what type?' questions, some qualitative 'Why?' and 'How?' questions are very valuable.

Box 4.1 gives an example of how well-chosen questions about a regular event can help make choices and changes that improve the event in future.

BOX 4.1

IMPROVING AN EVENT BASED ON ANSWERS TO QUESTIONS

For several years a city art gallery and museum held an annual reception called the Patrons' Evening. The idea was to thank past supporters, make new friends and give an annual update of the organisation's work and achievements. It was also a very successful vehicle for fundraising, helped keep up morale and contributed to the strategic need to maintain and increase its support base, so as to be able to undertake increasing amounts of conservation work and to commission new works.

The evening was evaluated carefully each year and several improvements were made, based on the answers to certain questions, including the following:

- **What proportion of those invited actually respond and attend?** Initially a 50 per cent response rate was assumed and too few were invited; in fact the answer was nearer 25 per cent, so in future years it was possible to adjust the number of initial invitations and plan the numbers for the event quite accurately.

- **Why do certain people respond positively?** It was found that telephoned or personalised invitations produced the best response, and so this method was used increasingly, especially for key guests.

- **What motivates guests to come?** It was found that they wanted to meet front-line staff more than management, and so curators, restorers and gallery attendants were invited. (This also helped to make staff feel more involved and motivated themselves.)

➡

- **What do guests particularly enjoy?** It was found that the opportunity to look 'behind the scenes' was particularly popular, so demonstrations of conservation techniques were included and a small number of objects not normally on display were brought out of storage specially for the event.

- **Is the timing and location good?** The event was held in the city centre just before a major religious festival, and the answer was that this worked well since people from all over the region could combine the trip with their shopping and other preparations.

4.2.3 The basis for useful questions

The most useful sets of questions to ask are those which include the following five elements:

- implications for practical choices (and making improvements)
- accountability to stakeholders (and relevance to stakeholders' objectives)
- measurement of degree of success (or failure/weakness)
- aiding understanding (of why certain things lead to success)
- comparison.

The first two are the key elements, and the others follow. The first question is probably the most important as it recognises the fact that evaluation is only worth doing if you can use the results to improve your practice. You will meet different models of evaluation below, but in each case these five elements remain.

ACTIVITY 4.3

From within your own organisation, or another with which you are familiar, think of an example of an event, campaign or specific set of activities aimed at winning resources or support. (It's probably best if the example you choose is relatively self-contained but with a degree of internal complexity.)

Jot down a list of up to eight questions about your chosen example to which you would like to have answers.

1 _____

2 _____

3 _____

4 _____

5 _____

---

6 _____

7 _____

8 _____

Now use the table below to check your questions against the five elements for useful evaluation suggested above. Put a score in each cell on a range of 1, for little or no correspondence between the question and the element, to 5 for maximum correspondence.

	Element				
Question	Implications for practical choices	Accountability to stakeholders	Measurement of degree of success	Aiding understanding	Comparison
1					
2					
3					
4					
5					
6					
7					
8					

Finally, review the wording of each question and add or suggest additional questions so that the whole list more usefully reflects these elements. As a result of this exercise you should have a sharper sense of what makes a good evaluative question in your situation.

_____

_____

_____

_____

4.3 EVALUATION: MONITORING, REVIEW AND ASSESSMENT

Terms like evaluation, monitoring, review and assessment are used in everyday language, often with overlapping meanings. This section offers a reminder and an exploration of the different meanings attached to these terms in this course: as stages in a loop, from finding out what is happening to doing something about it.

Monitoring

Monitoring implies watching for things going wrong. It requires continuous information gathering – for example, recording bookings coming in for a fundraising dinner or participants registering for a sponsored parachute jump. It is a mechanism for collecting information. However, we need to be cautious about using only monitoring information to come to conclusions. For example, routine monitoring of registrations for an annual event might reveal that these are running at 10 per cent more than the equivalent period last year. If you have just undertaken a substantial direct marketing exercise, the temptation is to assume that *that* is paying dividends. But you do not *know* why people chose to register for this event at that point in time without asking them. So monitoring of activities is clearly a part of the process of evaluation, but it is not the whole picture.

Review

Review implies both looking back and looking again, examining the whole situation in as broad a way as possible, including consideration of the interests of different stakeholders. The example given in Box 4.1, about the museum's Patrons' Evening, involved review (looking back, asking questions about what proportion responded to invitations etc.). Faced with indications that opportunities for improvement exist, we will *review* the situation – look at what has been happening and think again about whether this is the best way of operating. Again, this is part of the evaluative process.

Assessment

If the process of review indicates that things need to change, you may make some *assessment* of what the options are. In the case of the Patrons' Evening, where guests said that they liked the idea of looking 'behind the scenes', the museum might consider running guided tours for key guests during the evening, to show the vast number of acquisitions in store and requiring display space. Or it might make and run a video showing the preparation that needs to be done before a new exhibition is opened. After further assessment of the costs and benefits of these options, the museum may put one of them into operation. There will then be a need to monitor and review the impact of this change at the next event. So what starts as a one-off observation can turn into a continuous process of monitoring, review and assessment (see Table 4.1).

Table 4.1 Monitoring, review and assessment		
	Looks at	**In order to**
Monitoring	Present operation/context	Modify immediately
Review	Past or current project	Decide whether/how to repeat
Assessment	Options for future	Decide on plan

4.4 LOOKING AT WHAT? INPUTS, ACTIVITIES, OUTPUTS AND OUTCOMES

When undertaking any evaluation we need to define carefully the limits of the activity to be evaluated. This is particularly true when evaluating resource-winning and support-winning activities. Is it an evaluation of just one event or campaign or of all activities aimed at generating resources from other organisations, or of the whole of the organisation's fundraising or public relations strategy? All these possibilities would lead to valid evaluation work, but each would involve different methods and measures.

Different stakeholders place different emphases on the importance of different aspects of a project. These differences of emphasis can be reflected in a different focus of evaluation. As an example, if we set out to evaluate a meal which we have prepared for guests, we might focus on one or more of the following aspects:

- **Inputs**. The focus here is on all the resources needed to carry out the task. How much time did it take? Did we have the right ingredients? What did it cost in fuel? Was the cooker adequate? Was the kitchen well designed?

- **Activities and processes**. The focus here is on how the task was done. How did we go about the process of cooking the food?

- **Outputs**. The focus here is on the product or level of service. Was the intended amount of food produced? Was it the right temperature? Was it nutritious?

- **Outcomes**. The focus here is on whether the intended effect was produced. Did our guests eat their meal? Did they enjoy it? Was the food what they wanted?

Each focus is a legitimate one for evaluation, but it helps to be clear at the start of an evaluation process which focus is of particular concern. Evaluation can be problematic if different people have different perceptions about its focus.

The answers to the questions asked within each focus are meaningful at different levels. Questions about inputs tell you more about the *economy* of your management. Questions about outputs are revealing about the *efficiency* of your conversion of inputs into outputs. Questions about outcomes say something about the *effectiveness* of the whole operation. And your activities and processes can demonstrate your *ethics* at work. In the next section we explore how these different focuses of evaluation fit into the various *types* of evaluation which voluntary and non-profit organisations undertake.

ACTIVITY 4.4

Choose a fundraising initiative in which you have been involved in some way.

Under each of the four focus headings below, list up to three examples of relevant indicators which you could use in an evaluation.

Inputs:

_____

_____

_____

Activities and processes:

_____

_____

_____

Outputs:

_____

_____

_____

Outcomes:

_____

_____

_____

Here is a worked example based on a local charity's Christmas Draw:

Inputs. How much effort did it take to get prizes donated? How expensive was the ticket printing? Did we need to buy any prizes?

Activities and processes. How did we organise ticket sales and the return of money? Was the draw conducted fairly? How long did we have the tickets on sale?

Outputs. Were the prizes sufficiently attractive? Were the books of tickets priced appropriately? Did ticket sellers receive any acknowledgement?

> **Outcomes.** How much money did we raise? Did we manage to get any local media coverage for the draw? Did we get any publicity for our wider work?

4.4.1 Types of evaluation

The main types of evaluation are summarised in Table 4.2.

Table 4.2	Types of evaluation	
Type of evaluation	**Focus**	**Answers about ...**
Performance	Relationships between inputs and outputs	Economy and efficiency
Process	Activities	Links between how things are done and what happens
Impact	Relationships between outputs and outcomes	Effectiveness
Strategic	Are we doing the right thing?	Aims or overall goals of organisation
Composite	Mixture of above	Some or all of the above

Now let's work through each of the five listed in more detail to get a clearer idea of what is involved.

Performance evaluation

Performance evaluation takes the specific objectives and targets set for a project, event or initiative and seeks to measure the extent to which these are achieved in terms of both quantity and quality. The kind of financial evaluation we discussed in Session 3 of this book is a form of performance evaluation. It often focuses on issues like value for money and is the kind most commonly sought by funders. With the growth in contracts and service agreements, this approach is often linked to *performance indicators* (again a concept we have touched on in Session 3). In the context of contracts or service agreements these are tools used to evaluate specific aspects of the service which are usually agreed by both parties before the contract is signed.

To evaluate resource-winning activities in this way means first setting measures of performance specifically for them. You should attempt to specify these as *well-defined* objectives – so that it is in principle possible to tell when they have been achieved. We will look further at performance measures later in this session.

Process evaluation

Process evaluation involves asking questions about how particular aspects of the organisation work and will look for links between how things are done and what happens. Often such an approach will look for good practice. This might entail making comparisons with proven techniques or systems in other organisations. An example is the benchmarking approach discussed in Session 3.

Impact evaluation

Impact evaluation concerns whether outcomes are achieved (the intended effect of our work). Was there any significant impact? Were there any unintended effects? It might look at the extent of donor/supporter satisfaction with particular events or whether anything significant has changed as a direct result of activities. When goals or aims are unclear, it can be difficult to relate them to actual outcomes.

Strategic evaluation

A strategic evaluation asks questions about the overall purposes and goals of the project or organisation. Is it doing the right thing? Sometimes this is a response to changes in the organisation's environment, like a major change of government policy in terms of grant funding.

Sometimes the purpose for which the organisation was established is no longer relevant because society has changed or medical advances have changed the pattern of disease.

Composite evaluation

Evaluations are rarely clear-cut in practice and often it is necessary to use a mixture of approaches. This is because issues of performance, process, impact and strategy are often interrelated. For example, an evaluation of performance may well raise questions about an organisation's overall fundraising strategy. Similarly, a performance evaluation may reveal aspects of an organisation's practices and processes which need to be improved. Asking questions in one area can raise questions about activities in another area.

ACTIVITY 4.5

What type of evaluation would you suggest in the following situations?

(a) An arts organisation has recently tried a new method of advertising its events. They now wish to know if this has been successful in attracting more people to their performances.

(b) You have recently employed a member of your fundraising team to work both on direct fundraising and on developing and supporting local fundraising committees. You want to know how her time and effort is allocated between these two aspects of the job.

_____

_____

(c) You set up a volunteer group in your organisation and you want to know whether it is successful. How useful was the induction and training given? What roles are the volunteers most comfortable with? What has been less successful?

_____

_____

(a) performance – has the advertising worked?; (b) process – the way the team member works; (c) impact – how effective has the initiative been? There are areas of overlap here, but clarity of purpose helps ensure the right choice of evaluation.

4.5 MEASURES OF PERFORMANCE

The simplest way of ensuring that resource-winning objectives are well defined is to express them in terms of *measures of performance* with *targets for a given time period* that are in principle achievable.

For example, a measure of performance for a particular fundraising event could be the total amount of money raised, with a corresponding target set at 10 per cent more than last year, so the objective would then be 'to raise at least 10 per cent more than last year'. Or, in a case where there is a specific requirement for enough resources to run a particular programme or a building, the measure of performance could be the amount spent on fundraising, and the corresponding target set at 20 per cent of the programme budget. Then the objective would be 'to keep the costs of fundraising down to 20 per cent of the programme budget or less'. These are both well-defined objectives in that one could expect to see whether or not they had been achieved. The SMART criteria of being specific, measurable, agreed, realistic and time-related apply here as they do to all objectives.

Every separate event or initiative can have its own particular quantitative measures attached. However, it helps when constructing these measures, and making sure that they are appropriate, to think of them falling within four general types: measures of effectiveness, efficiency, economy and ethics.

4.5.1 Measuring effectiveness

Measures of *effectiveness* are designed to show directly how effectively the goals of the activity (and hence the aims of the organisation as a whole) are being met. So if the goal is raising money, the measure would simply be the amount of money raised; if the goal is to make the funding more secure and long term, then a measure of effectiveness could be the proportion of funds coming from tax-efficient forms of giving such as the UK's GiftAid, payroll giving and other regular sources of income.

Depending on how broad an evaluation is being undertaken, measures of effectiveness can be measures of *output* or of *outcomes*. This can in practice lead to two rather different kinds of effectiveness measure – though they can both often be expressed usefully as percentages of some standard or desired level or as rates of growth. The first kind measures how well the immediate task is performed – whether the agreed number of press releases is produced on time; how many groups have been contacted for pledges to participate in a fundraising event; whether an advertisement is fully understood. The second measures how effectively the desired outcome has been achieved – this could just mean how much money has been obtained, but it could also be a question of whether the desired proportion of UK respondents signed a GiftAid declaration (or, elsewhere in the world, opted for an equivalent form of tax-effective giving). One specific effectiveness measure that should be noted is the net income from an event or activity (that is, funds raised *less* expenses). This is often called simply the *contribution*, though, as we shall see, the term 'contribution' can also be used for the extent to which a particular activity contributes to meeting an overall target.

Here, we are considering measuring the outcomes of a resource-winning activity, not the outcomes for the organisation as a whole or its other activities (such as service providing). 'Outcomes' in this sense are, of course, important to all fund raisers in making a case for support – but are of particular concern to those involved in applying or reporting to some organisational funders such as trusts and the Big Lottery Fund. It is extremely challenging to measure effectiveness at the whole-organisation level. You may find it hard to imagine how to measure the extent to which goals such as 'relieving child poverty' or 'ending world hunger' are met – and even demonstrating that, for example, increased participation rates in education or employment among a target population are a direct result of a particular intervention is very difficult. Measurement of this type introduces all sorts of problems to do with definitions, timescale and causality – but remains of understandable interest to funders. Ideally, however, even if we restrict attention to measuring the effectiveness of resource winning in such a context, this would include some notion of how appropriate to the overall aims of the organisation was the type of resource gained.

4.5.2 Measuring efficiency

Measures of *efficiency* relate outputs (or outcomes) to resources used to achieve those outputs (or outcomes). They are typically in the form of a *ratio* of output (or outcome) to input. In the case of a fundraising event or method, the simplest efficiency ratio would be the amount of income raised divided by the cost of raising it. This is termed the *simple fundraising ratio* – or sometimes just the *ratio*. As we have seen in Session 3, this apparently simple statistic becomes a lot more complicated once you start thinking about it.

In fact this ratio varies a lot according to factors such as whether the money is being raised by a well-established organisation or 'brand', or a new organisation or appeal, whether the cause is an emotive and popular one, and so on. It also varies for different types of activities: dinner dances might yield 3:1 whereas work on legacies might bring in 30:1 over a period. So, different guide ratios are appropriate in different cases. At the margins, it may be justifiable to spend £9 to raise £10!

It is important not to be rigid in the use of such ratios, and to be careful how they are used. There is a big difference between the 'external' use of ratios for comparing one organisation with another (5:1 may make sense for large aid agencies but not for specialist local organisations, where what is feasible depends on the region, the cause and other local factors) and the 'internal' use in comparing one region of the same organisation with another, this year with previous years, or efforts to raise money by similar methods from different target groups. For 'internal' use, you can to some extent choose your own target ratios and use the information about what has been achieved by different activities in different parts of the organisation for internal management purposes (deciding which activities to continue or modify, where to put in extra resources, and so on).

However, there is less leeway over the 'external' use of the fundraising ratio. To some extent it is not a question of what is feasible, but of what is 'proper'. Spending a large proportion of the organisation's income on fundraising may not be acceptable to potential donors (or to other stakeholders), even if as a result the total raised and thus the effectiveness with which the operational goals can be pursued, is increased. And donors and stakeholders may well have a notion that a ratio of 5:1, for example, is what is 'proper'.

4.5.3 Measuring economy

Economy measures are useful when it is known what outputs have to be achieved (i.e. intermediary results which facilitate the 'outcomes' for which the organisation is striving through its work). An organisation may have specific ongoing responsibilities to meet, say a building to run or a certain number of projects to keep going. The objective could then be to do so at least cost, or, to recast this as a well-defined objective, to bring the cost down to or

Economy is another apparently simple measure which gets more complicated when you start exploring it. For example, many charities rely heavily on the work of volunteers in both fundraising and programme delivery. However, there can be a tendency to think that volunteers should be virtually free – that is, the cost of recruiting and supporting them should be kept to a very low target figure. This is using an *economy*-type measure. This may conflict with *effectiveness* in that poorly resourced and supported volunteers may not be so effective at whatever they are volunteering to do, which may include telemarketing, door-to-door fundraising, and so on. Since they have a choice of where to volunteer, they may also leave if they are poorly served!

below a set target level within a given time period. An economy measure is thus a measure of the *input*. The actual measure could be cost in terms of money, hours of volunteer time, or some other resource. On the whole, however, economy measures are useful by themselves only in very limited cases.

4.5.4 Measuring ethics

Ethics, the last of these four Es, refers to the impact of the organisation on society. You can measure ethical impact on a number of fronts – environmental considerations, treatment of paid staff and volunteers, adherence to equal opportunities practice, and how responsible the organisation's stewardship of its resources has been in terms of the public interest. As we have seen in Book 1, ethics is an extremely important consideration in developing fundraising practice and management, and so this measure needs to be prioritised in evaluation work.

You may have noticed that as we have moved through the four Es our perspective for measuring performance has changed its focus. Economy and efficiency are concerned with internal measures – how good the organisation is at getting things done. Effectiveness and ethics, however, widen the focus to take in measurements and norms which may be outside the direct control of the organisation.

4.5.5 Some difficulties and limitations of using measures of performance

It is more usually the case that we need to use more than one of these four types of measures at the same time, though unless one measure has precedence, we can hit the problem that the different types tend to conflict with each other! Most obviously, aiming for economy or efficiency may not, by itself, be the best way to achieve increases in the amount of resource gained and hence growth in the organisation's activities or more effective achievement of its overall goals. The additional pressure on staff and volunteers may endanger its ethical output.

Undoubtedly quantitative information can be powerful: 'the results speak for themselves!' However the 'results' provided by quantitative information need to be contextualised, as demonstrated in Box 4.2 below.

BOX 4.2

GREENFORCE'S GREEN SHOOTS CAMPAIGN

GreenForce is an environmental organisation which launched a new series of national fundraising advertisements, using direct mail, text and email messaging to targeted supporters. In the three months following the launch there was a 50 per cent increase in ➡

---

the number of donations and a 10 per cent increase in the average amount donated, compared with the previous three months and the same three-month period in previous years. So, should the new advertisements be judged a 'success'?

'Scanning' of the context in which your fundraising operates can inform and enrich your evaluation, even if it muddies the 'simple truth' of the quantitative data. One of the big problems in evaluation is 'causality' – the linking of results to reasons. Taking the GreenForce example, an evaluation which reported that the organisation's advertisements worked, because donations went up by 50 per cent in the month following them, could be on the wrong track: perhaps the campaign coincided with a major oil spillage disaster which resulted in significant donation increases for all environmental organisations. In that instance, the qualitative angle (awareness of what's happening and what to take into account) could have helped to frame more appropriate quantitative information gathering and analysis.

Some people label quantitative data as a *hard* evaluation approach, and qualitative data as a *soft* approach. These labels can be unhelpful – especially if they give too much weight to the absolute amount of money raised rather than the circumstances in which this was achieved. What matters in evaluation is an appropriate balance.

ACTIVITY 4.6

Look back to the fundraising activity/event which you used as your example in Activity 4.3. Identify which of the following measures of performance were applied/ could apply in that situation:

Effectiveness

Efficiency

Economy

Ethics

Are there any conflicts between these measures?

Are there any particular 'contextual' factors which might have influenced the results of this particular event/campaign?

_____

_____

_____

4.6 SUMMARY

Here is a summary of the main learning points from this session:

- Evaluation allows organisations to exercise accountability and to make better choices and improvements.
- Stakeholder analysis helps determine what questions to ask in an evaluation aimed at accountability.
- Identifying which decisions you have control over helps determine what questions to ask in an evaluation aimed at improvement.
- Useful evaluation asks questions about:
  - implications for practical choices (and making improvements)
  - accountability to stakeholders (and relevance to stakeholders' objectives)
  - measurement of degree of success (or failure/weakness)
  - aiding understanding (e.g. of reasons for success)
  - comparison.
- Monitoring keeps a watch for things going wrong by collecting information during the course of an activity and comparing against target.
- Review looks back to examine the whole of a situation in as broad a way as possible.
- Assessment examines and compares options for future activity.
- Evaluation can focus on inputs (linked to economy), activities and processes (linked to ethics), outputs (linked to efficiency) and outcomes (linked to effectiveness). Each focus is legitimate, but the evaluation will be more successful if it is clear which focus is of particular concern.
- The main types of evaluation are:
  - performance evaluation, concentrating on the relationship between inputs and outputs
  - process evaluation, concentrating on activities
  - impact evaluation, concentrating on the relationship between outputs and outcomes
  - strategic evalation, concentrating on whether the organisation is doing the right things

- composite evaluation, combining a mixture of some or all of the other types.

- Measures of performance fall within the general headings of the '4 Es': economy (doing things cheaply), effectiveness (doing the right things), efficiency (doing things right), and ethics (doing 'right').

REFERENCES

ACEVO (2004) *Funding our Future: Core Costs Revisited* (3rd edn), London, Association of Chief Executives of Voluntary Organisations.

Belbin, R.M. (1996) *Team Roles at Work*, London, Butterworth-Heinemann.

Burnett, K. (2002) *Relationship Fundraising: A Donor-Based Approach to the Business of Raising Money*, San Francisco CA, Jossey-Bass with the White Lion Press.

Flory, P. (2001) 'Data Basics', *Third Sector*, 28 June.

Funnell, R. and Darker, C. (2007) 'The rise and rise of prospect research', *Professional Fundraising*, April, pp. 26–27.

Gaskin, K. (2003) *A Choice Blend* [online], London, Institute for Volunteering Research, http://www.ivr.org.uk/choiceblend.htm (accessed 24 July 2007).

Handy, C. (1976) *Understanding Organizations* (1st edn), Harmondsworth, Penguin.

Handy, C. (2004) *Understanding Voluntary Organisations*, Harmondsworth, Penguin.

Harrison, I. (2003) 'Scottish charities in fury over database', *The Sunday Post*, 6 July.

Hibberd, B. and Evatt, A. (2004) 'Mapping information flows: a practical guide', *The Information Management Journal*, January/ February, pp. 58–64, [online], http://scientific.thomson.com/ quantum2/media/pdfs/mapping_info_flows.pdf (accessed 20 September 2007).

Huczynski, A. and Buchanan, D. (2003) *Organisational Behaviour* (5th edn), London, Prentice Hall.

Institute of Fundraising (2007) 'Fundratios Project: Trends in Giving' [online], http://www.institute-of-fundraising.org.uk/ informationaboutfundraising/forfundraisers/researchdirectory/ fundratiosprojecttrendsingiving.htm (accessed 20 September 2007).

Janis, I.J. (1972) *Victims of Groupthink*, Boston, Houghton Mifflin.

Kakabadse, A., Ludlow, R. and Vinnicombe, S. (1988) *Working in Organisations*, London, Penguin.

Kanter, B. (2002) *Database Planning: Leading with Needs not Solutions* [online], TechSoup NPO Story, http://www.techsoup.org/ learningcenter/databases/page5215.cfm?cg=searchterms&sg=Kanter (accessed 24 July 2007).

Lucey, T. (1998) *Management Information Systems* (8th edn), London, Letts Educational.

Maslow, A.H. (1954) *Motivation and Personality*, New York, Harper and Row.

Mintzberg, H. (1973) *The Nature of Managerial Work*, New York, Harper and Row.

NCVO/CAF (2006) *UK Giving 2004/5 Results of the 2004/5 Survey of Individual Charitable Giving in the UK* [online], http://www.cafonline.org/pdf/UKGiving200405.pdf (accessed 20 September 2007).

Sargeant, A. and Jay, E. (2004) *Fundraising Management: Analysis, Planning and Practice*, London, Routledge.

Schein, E. (1996) in Pugh, D.S. (ed.) *Writers on Organisations*, Harmondsworth, Penguin, pp. 167–71.

Tuckman, B.W. (1965) 'Developmental sequences in small groups', *Psychological Bulletin*, vol. 63, no. 6, pp. 384–99.

ACKNOWLEDGEMENTS

Grateful acknowledgement is made to the following sources for permission to reproduce material within this product.

Text

Pp. 60–1 London Advice Services Alliance; *pp. 105–6* Harrison, I. (2003) 'Scottish charities in fury over database', *The Sunday Post*, 6 July 2003. Extract from *The Sunday Post* © DC Thomson & Co Ltd. *Box 1.3*: Lasa Information Systems Team (2002) 'A quick guide to planning your database'. Copyright © 2002 Lasa Information Systems Team; Box 3.3: Harrison, I. 'Scottish charities in fury over database', The Sunday Post 6 July 2003, © D.C.Thomson & Co., Ltd;

Tables

Table 2.2: Taken with permission from www.belbin.com; *Table 3.6*: The Institute of Fundraisers, 'Fundraising cost effectiveness', Annual Fund Ratios Exercise © The Institute of Fundraisers and the Centre for Interfirm Comparisons;